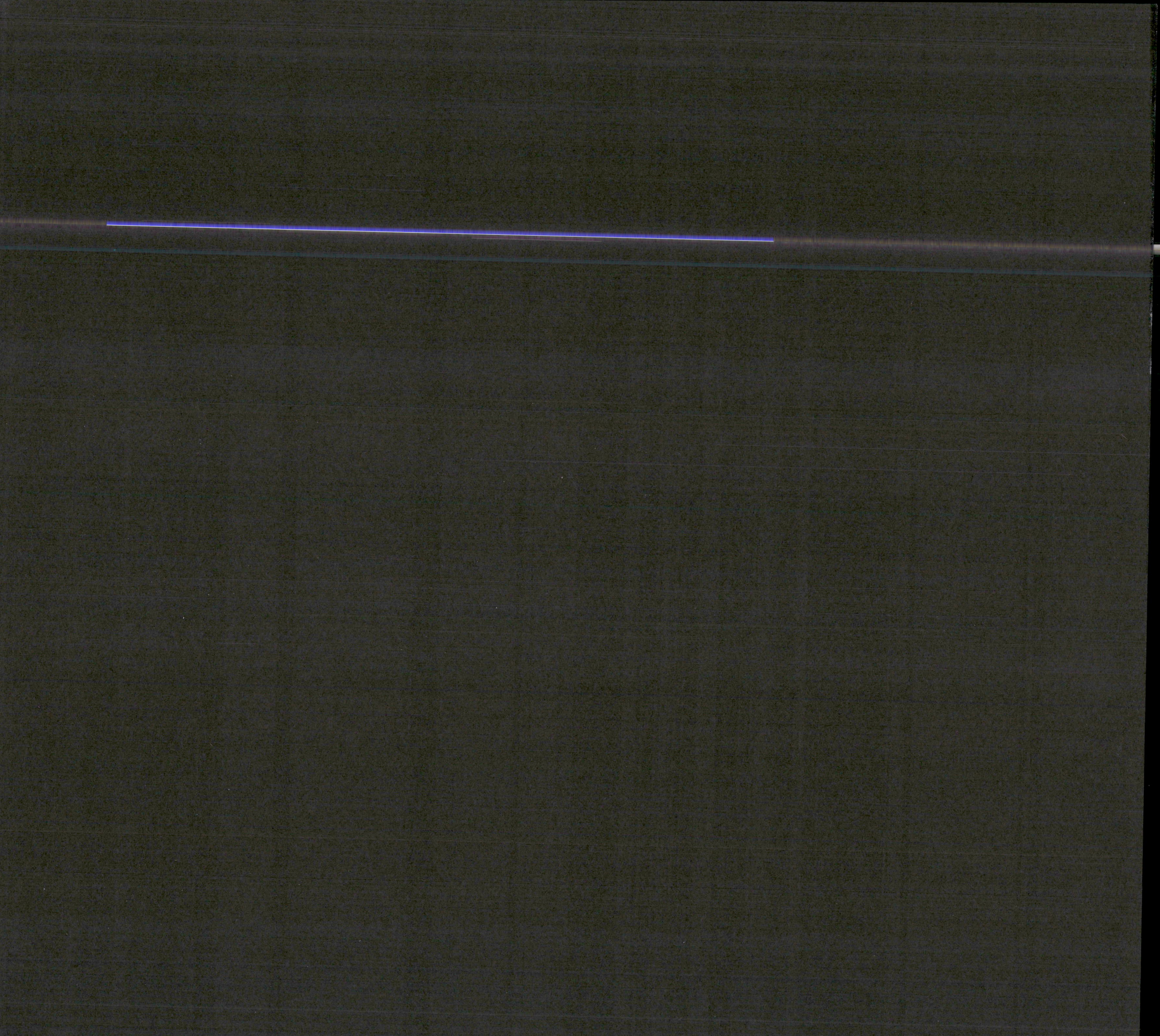

superdiscount

the unit architects

essays by

Wally Olins
Wayne K. Homren
Matthias Henkel
Graham Vickers
Wolfgang Pauser
Alison J. Clarke

edited by

section.a art.design.consulting

09 prefaces

14 editorial

20 shopping

88 banking

112 working

contents

152 warehousing

176 exhibiting

208 living

234 visions

252 appendix

Conceptualizing a book for the architecture office the unit was a challenging task in every respect. For section.a, an art and design consulting company that is constantly concerned with the subject of "cultural identity" in its own work, the main objective lay in developing a concept that was suitable for specialists in architectural corporate identity. The cooperation with members of section.d, who have been longstanding partners of the unit and who are also CI experts, was indispensable to this project.

Although the unit's work is characterized by a high degree of pragmatism within the confines of the retail world, the resulting architecture is appealing and exudes great charisma.

The usual box-like concrete structures suddenly become shining landmarks, which not only redefine anonymous landscapes on the outskirts of a city, but also set a new standard of Austrian shopping architecture. However, the unit's architecture does not aspire to timelessness. It appeals to average consumers and addresses their living and shopping experience at a sophisticated level. Once the shopping world has outlived its purpose, its shell will disappear. The consumer world is fast-paced, and the unit provides the corresponding architecture, unsentimental and transitory.

In keeping with this attitude, we did not conceive an aura-based architecture book. Instead, we concentrated on the themes that the unit addresses with their work. The world of consumption and the anonymous consumer have been given just as much space in this book as the sample projects. Divided into chapters such as shopping, banking, working, warehousing, exhibiting and living, the projects can be viewed from the perspective of the respective contexts; they aren't discussed for their own sake.

The individual chapters feature the photographic work of Pascal Petignat, which focuses on the person and his behavior within a specific context instead of the architecture. This subtle handling of observation shows our everyday world and its comedy without denying the main characters (of consumption and the related architectural worlds) the respect they deserve.

The essays written by acclaimed authors, all of them experts in fields such as psychology, ethnology, numismatics or design theory, enrich and complete the themes that were redefined by the unit. Although the articles do not address the unit's work directly, the theoretical contributions make observation possible at another level, giving the scope of an architecture book a new dimension.

Wally Olins, one of the worlds' most respected CI and branding specialists, wrote the exposition on the overall subject of Architecture and Corporate Design. In his essay, he describes the development of the "architecture as branding" from its beginnings to the present day and he also discusses the corresponding surroundings, which are decisive for the identity of every company.

David Lewis, an English psychologist and the chairman of David Lewis Consultancy, a respected company in the field, discusses the development and authenticity of the "new" consumer in the shopping chapter.

The American financial analyst and coin expert Wayne Homren analyses the history and development of money, as well as trust, which he considers to be the most important parameters for a bank building.

In the working chapter, the German ethnologist and archaeologist Matthias Henkel presents his views on architecture and (office) work from an anthropological and cultural-historical perspective.

Graham Vickers, the British writer specialising in design, architecture and advertising addresses the fundamental thoughts behind warehousing, logistics and goods distribution and seeks to establish whether every building is automatically architecture in his contribution on the subject of warehousing.

The Austrian Wolfgang Pauser, a freelance essayist on the culture of consumption and the fine arts, describes the showcase's progress from museums to theme stores in the exhibiting section.

In the living chapter, the British design theorist Alison Clarke explores the essential interaction between the inhabitant and his place of residence as well as the aesthetic and social aspects of living.

Additionally, the book features a selection of projects by the unit in each of the six chapters that complement the written and photographic contributions. The final section on visions offers a look at projects that were not realized or are still to be built.

SUPERDISCOUNIT endeavors to inform the interested public on the many fields the unit addresses. It also strives to offer new impetus and ideas, and give the discussion of architecture greater depth. We hope we were successful in our endeavors.

section.a
Vienna, 2003

It is somewhat bizarre to try to describe your own work with words. Images and language don't agree with each other. Nonetheless, I can try to say something about the mantle of my work – "discreet fascination through manipulation."

PERCEIVING COHERENCE – Let us start with the fundamentals: First of all, style is a matter of coherence to me. This can easily be seen in the luxury product lines of multinational fashion companies (such as Prada), which when examined closely is the continuing implementation of knowledge that isn't really that new: The particularities of shops and services can no longer be separated from the design of the shops or sales points (you only have to think of Mc Donald's or the various gas station chains). Perceiving this coherence triggers a certain, although diffuse awareness: this is an own "world"! The potential buyers feel the desire for identification, acceptance and integration. The often-apostrophized "desire to shop" is the result: participation by appropriation.

A SINGLE FAMILY HOUSE AS AN OUTLET – "Corporate Design" (CD) and "Corporate Identity" (CI) are not new facts; only the term is a more recent creation. If you think of churches, gas stations and airlines, then these facts have existed for a long time. But our intentions and understanding of ourselves reach further: even a seemingly insignificant one-family house bears CI marks. For this reason, it makes no difference to us whether the client wants to redesign a few hundred outlets or if a client want to build an "outlet" for family purposes, namely a house. The development process and preparation of the prototype are the same.

Ultimately, the difference between a good and a bad shop lies in how well the sales strategy matches the company philosophy and whether the architecture for the corresponding image can be found. It is the image the "shop" conveys that the customer takes home and which offers him topographical guidance.
It was only after Prada and Rem Kolhaas that architects understood that future clients will primarily be companies, meaning those business entities that follow a strict "Economy of Awareness," (Franck) in presenting their products.

ASPECTS OF ARCHITECTURAL EXPERIENCE – Architects are aware of the stylistic, the technical and maybe even of the economic aspects of their designs. But they know very little about the forms and construction strategies that are responsible for triggering associations and connotations that might possibly be decisive in a buying decision. The field of emotions triggered by structures is still Terra Incognita to the architect. And it is noticeable that very few designers take this mental and physiological effect into consideration for their forms and surface vocabularies. Of course: what isn't considered can't work. Product-specific design phenomena are primarily perceived via an experience. However, this "experience" is dependent on dispositives and settings. This is the point of departure for "Shop Design."

CREATING NEW PATTERNS OF SPEECH – Architecture cannot remain aloof from generally valid language codes. The attempt to create individual patterns of speech doesn't take place in an empty space. The development of individual patterns of speech (and the thus generated possibility of finding new ways to read familiar things) lives from being able to read new things in older things and hence see them in a new way. With some conscientiousness, it should be possible to catalog a "new" vocabulary. Then the possibility arises of working with a language of images that conforms to the company and its products. It is only possible to realize architecture that serves the defined meaning, convictions and "philosophies" - form follows spirit!

How much can the customer be asked to remember and recognize – Companies insist on realizing ideas that conform to the product and the company (or let us say adequate ideas). A language of images that only complies with architecture would undermine this postulate. The question arises again: how can the customer and/or member keep recognizing the unmistakable product (or specific service)?

RETHINK DEFINITIONS OF QUALITY – It is ultimately a simple fact (that can be criticized) that companies aren't interested in presenting "the best quality objectively" without it being certain that the quality is also perceived to be the best by the customer subjectively. Modern quality measurement methods in the customer sector have exposed a common mistake made in the past: time and again, quality was determined from the point of view of the company, the subjective feeling (decisive for frequency and buying decisions) of the customer were neglected, never discussed, ignored.

It could be said that this is all a staged production, all only about appearances. But it is the appearances that are real. Nothing is left to chance. Customers are like birds: they have a feeling for masses. Birds follow other birds; I can watch them for hours. Customer psychology, getting to the bottom of that secret appeals to me.

That brings us to "manipulation." Translated literally it means: "handling," the way a carpenter handles a plane. It means knowing how to handle the plane. Architecture alone is too little. We need specialists and we use them. What is important is that the central interface be ours, we want to be in charge of directing. It is astonishing to see how many companies there are in which advertising, marketing, sales and shop architecture no nothing about each other. This is harmful for all: for the company, the customers and the architecture.

We understand by observing: how do customers walk through a supermarket? What annoys them? Why did they reach for that product instead of the other? The customer will explain in simple words. I follow them for hours and observe them. Design knowledge is informed experience.

It creates a very particular type of excitement to decipher a certain quality within the increasing quantity of buying and shopping actions. The same happens to me when I listen to the music of Johann Sebastian Bach: I hear successive polyphony, variations along a line – it is precisely these additive phenomena that fascinate me. Those who ask me about the one favorite task I would like to complete receive a surprising answer: a small, quiet chapel far removed from any form of material consumption – of course it should immediately be noted that the church as a company of the largest order with a few million outlets has needed a CI overhaul for a while.

IDEAS INCLUDED – When we brief new clients, we talk about emotions, attitudes and postures. Form and material are of secondary importance initially. We make sure that the concept, the idea is ours. We aren't psychoanalysts with the gift of bringing the client's innermost thoughts to the surface. We cannot promise to satisfy the egos of strangers. Surfaces are only generated very late in an understandable intersubjective process: materials and emotions have to support each other and give each other presence reciprocally. However, the true core of our work isn't calculable. That is the fascination of the central idea this book is dedicated to.
We live from the strength of the projects we realize: knowledge and imagination are important but the strength to give an idea presence (in a company-adequate) way is decisive. Ultimately it is only the result, the realized final product that can "satisfy" the public.

Are we satisified with what we do? Are we successful? To quote Ralph Waldo Emerson: "To laugh often and much, to win the respect of intelligent people and the affection of children, to earn the appreciation of honest critics and endure the betrayal of false friends, to appreciate beauty, to find the best in others, to leave the world a bit better, whether by a healthy child, a garden patch, or a redeemed social condition; to know even one life has breathed easier because you have lived. This is to have succeeded! "
We are on the way to being successful.

Wolfgang Bürgler,
Vienna, 2003

preface

For us, the unit is a platform from which we can take comprehensive action at many levels. The office name symbolises the creation of a designed "work piece" – characterised and discussed by specialists active who are active in a broad range of humanistic fields. This open handling of architecture leads to a wide-ranging analysis of themes that influence the construction project. Our spaces are given life by their contents, they become identity bearers, a linking element for communication and discussion.

Uniqueness, resulting from design parameters and the social relationship patterns of the pervading social spirit, gives the projects a stronger emotional presence.

Rational building requirements are combined with a language of forms that is as timeless as possible. Minimalism isn't a primary architectural goal; instead it is the unavoidable opposite pole to the nervousness of today's consumer society.

These simple structures avoid inflation and the devaluation of symbols; they focus the eye on the fundamentals. A reduced architectural box emerges, conveying archaic calm in the hubbub of shopping, in the bustle of social interaction, making it unmistakable and strong.

The monolith floating in the infinite realm of space in Stanley Kubrick's "2001" is the best example of emotional architecture. This built endless space refuses to convey a language of concurring architectural images. It stimulates the observer to focus on what has been built, the unknown tempts the observer to touch and enter it. Construction is an integral matter for us. It influences its users, the observer and its surroundings. With the aid of our artistic and organisational reasoning, we try to create an unmistakable place of strength.

If it can be built, this kind of architecture supports the emotions desired by the users. No aspect of life remains unaffected by this type of creative quality. Whether it is built for living, shopping, loving, dining, drinking, exhibits, playing or thinking, all experiences can be improved and emphasised with architecture.

The projects true strength lies in how they work with each other. The reactions of many people at different levels help create unmistakable buildings.

The projects presented here are an excerpt of our lives as they proceed. New directions will define the way. Our architecture should be an encouragement for further development.
I hope for the culture and future of our country that open competitions and independent juries will once again become the only criteria for the creation of good architecture.
I would like to thank my family, my friends, my clients, partners and participating colleagues for all the emotions that were felt.

Georg Petrovic
Vienna, 2003

Architecture as branding

The pyramids of Giza outside Cairo in Egypt are probably the best known pieces of corporate architecture the world has ever seen. They are over 4,500 years old, so they are certainly amongst the most enduring.

Nobody except a few experts now remembers who built them, but we all know why they were built – as personal and dynastic monuments to celebrate the power, influence and wealth of the various pharaohs who were interred within them. They were meant to last for an eternity and they have. Although the kings who built them are now forgotten, the pyramids remain a powerful symbol of Egypt's pharaonic era. They are also a remarkable commercial success, something the men who commissioned them could never have begun to comprehend. They are a mammoth tourist attraction bringing in a multitude of visitors every year. However much they originally cost, they must have repaid the investment a million times over in terms of income from tourists. It is no exaggeration to say that Egypt is at least partly symbolised in the world through the pyramids and they are so powerful a manifestation of Egypt that it's almost impossible to think of the country without them.

The pyramids are an integral part of the Egyptian national brand. They are unmistakeable, immutable, unique. They have all the branding strengths.

The pyramids represent in an extreme form the essence of corporate architecture – or in contemporary marketing jargon, the relationship of architecture and environment to the rest of the brand mix.

But the pyramids are not unique. Over millennia sovereigns of every kind and every nation have sought to memorialise themselves, with buildings – and even cities. It's almost invidious to pick out one or two from so many centuries of design and construction. St. Petersburg, Versailles, Sans Souci just happen to be 17th and 18th century European examples. But the list is endless. Interestingly, the pyramids had religious as well as dynastic symbolism. And the tradition of religious environmental design is a global phenomenon. From Angkor Wat in Cambodia to Hagia Sophia in Byzantium and St Peter's in Rome – religious buildings are ubiquitous as prime movers in embracing the faithful.

Corporate architecture played a role recently, in the tragic events of 9/11. The Twin Towers became a symbol both of the catastrophe itself and of the American national will to rebuild and recover. So it's pretty big stuff.

On the face of it, there doesn't seem to be much connection between this kind of architecture and branding as we see it today. After all isn't branding about the obsessive repetition of a simple, often extravagant claim expressed through a strapline or slogan with a distinctive symbol and some colours plastered more or less at random over everything in sight? Isn't branding just the crassest and most vulgar manifestation of our commercially dominated society?

Well, when you get up close, branding is much more complex than that.

The clearest way to understand a brand is to look at it through the four vectors by which it manifests itself. They are the brand's four senses. Brands are almost always a mix of product, communication, behaviour and environment or architecture. Often one or other of these vectors dominates the brand mix.

The product is what the organisation makes or sells. Communication is how it tells people about itself and what it's doing. Behaviour is how everyone within the brand comports himself or herself in any interaction of any kind with any other individual or organisation and environment is where the organisation lives, where it works, where it makes and sells things – its buildings, plant, showrooms, offices.

Of these four vectors environment is much the most permanent. Products have a life cycle – a car lasts 5 or 10 years. Communication is ephemeral; advertising is here

today and gone tomorrow. Behaviour is literally of the moment. There is a single transaction between individuals – an airline steward serves you a drink. But environments go on for a long time. Often after the brand itself has disappeared. Sometimes, it seems almost for ever – just think of the pharaohs.

The brands most people immediately think of are communication driven – Coca-Cola, Red Bull, Persil, Kellogg's Corn Flakes, what are called, in the jargon of the marketing world, fast moving consumer goods. Specifically, most of these kinds of brands are advertising driven. The emotional stance of the product is seen through its communications, especially its TV, press and poster advertising. Advertising is the key. But even such communication based brands have a product of some kind.

Coca-Cola may be a maroon coloured fizzy liquid of, as some may think, little merit, intrinsic interest or distinction but when the formula was changed a few years ago, people noticed. The product mattered. It always does.

But there are plenty of brands where the product is much more complex than Coca-Cola and communication, although it remains significant is a subordinate factor in the brand mix. Objects that are complex to make are usually product led. Apple's iMac is a classic example – so is any car. It's the product that's at the core of the brand. What the car looks like, feels like to sit in and drive, how much it costs, how much fuel it uses, how the doors sound when you open and shut them, what the neighbours think when it's parked outside the front door and a thousand other little things around the product itself are the key to the automotive brand. Of course communication through advertising, environments like dealer showrooms and behaviour through after sales service are all very important but at the core for the product led brand is the product itself.

Then there are behaviourally led brands. There are plenty of organisations whose brand image emerges not so much through what they make (product), through the

images they use to promote themselves (communication) or where they live (environment) as through the way in which they behave. These are for the most part service organisations, like police forces, health authorities or in the commercial world mobile phone companies or airlines. Airlines are a classic example of behaviourally led brands. We almost always judge an airline on the basis of the service we received; not how long it took to fly from Vienna to New York, but what the experience was like from the moment we arrived at the airport till the time when we picked up our luggage.

Then there are environments, the vector with which this article is particularly concerned. Every organisation has offices, factories, dining rooms and other places in which staff live and carry out their work, and these have a powerful influence on the way employees see the organisation. But sometimes environments have a profound impact on the corporation's other audiences – especially customers. Architecture and interiors can have immense power for a brand.

In hotels, department stores and leisure centres the environment is the key vector through which the brand expresses itself. It presents the idea of the organisation in its entirety to its customers. One of the most attractive hotels I know is the Ciragan Palace in Istanbul. It is a former Ottoman palace located on the shores of the Bosphorus – on the edge of two continents. The service and food are of course superb. But it's the environment that really makes it so special. In retail stores like Bloomingdales in New York, or Harrods in London there are very few products on display that you can't buy somewhere else, often cheaper. What makes these stores unique is not what they sell or even how they sell it, although customer service is very important, but what they are like to be in – the atmosphere, or as we may prefer to call it – the environment. It's the total brand experience led by the environment that truly influences us. There are plenty of Harrods stores in airports, but to borrow a brand expression coined by Coca-Cola, they aren't The Real Thing. You'll only find The Real Harrods in its massive complex in Knightsbridge, London where the scale

of it all is simply overwhelming. The airport environments that Harrods takes over are just too commonplace, too ordinary to sustain the magic of Harrods flagship London store.

Then there are banks. Until very recently when internet banking began to take over, we all had to visit High Street bank branches, where a combination of behaviour and environment were the prime vectors influencing the brand. Banks have always invested very large amounts of time, money and ingenuity in their environments. Bank branches and especially their head offices have traditionally been a carefully calculated mixture of elements all designed to impress. I have spent a lot of time in the head office buildings of banks all over the world. Whatever their architectural style, they are all intended to overwhelm customers with a mix of wealth, good taste, (sometimes) and power. Many banks have very impressive collections of art brought together over many years and worth millions. Traditionally these have been hidden away somewhere in the directors' suites and only shown to clients the banks were particularly anxious to dazzle.

Size is also an important ingredient. The Hongkong and Shanghai Bank head office building in Hong Kong designed by Norman Foster and put up in the 1980s was the tallest building in the city until the Bank of China built something just a little bit taller a few years later. Coincidence? Hardly.

Like the ancient pharaohs, bank directors continue to build monuments to themselves and their organisations on the basis that they will exist for ever, even when the volatility of the market place in which they operate means that many of them disappear pretty quickly. The Bank of America building in San Francisco was put up in the heyday of its power (late 1960s) to emphasise Bank of America's position as the world's number one. The building is still there, a great San Francisco landmark, but the bank has moved out. The Bank of America is not quite what it was – although it's still as I write this, the world's number 3 banking player.

To gauge just how significant environmental design has traditionally been in bank branding you only need to walk along any High Street more or less anywhere. Bank facades almost always look a bit bigger, grander, more pompous and just a shade richer than their neighbours – the other shops, and this is no accident. The truth of the matter is that paying customers like us would have difficulty in trusting a bank that didn't spend a lot of money preening itself through its properties.

It's very tempting to think that all this is new – that the offices, factories and showrooms currently used to brand the corporation only have the most tenuous links with the palaces and castles created by and for princes, kings and emperors over the centuries. But in reality the sovereign used architecture and the environment for precisely the same purpose as corporations today – to impress, to propagandise, to seduce and to overawe both his own citizens and the neighbouring states – or as we might put it today, his own staff and customers, suppliers, shareholders and competitors.

The first corporations as opposed to temporal and spiritual rulers to use architecture and environments consciously and significantly to create a specific impression upon their publics and other stakeholders, as we might call them, were the railways. Britain was the pioneer in railways and it was in London that the great railway companies built monuments to themselves.

Major programmes were created by the great 19th century railway companies whose rolling stock, stations, liveried employees and advertising were also consciously designed to give a clear idea of each company's style and purpose and to bond together employees in the new and widely dispersed organisations. Sir John Betjeman the famous poet and architectural critic wrote in his book London's Historic Railway Stations[1], "The individuality of the great companies was expressed in styles of architecture, typography and liveries of engines and carriages even down to the knives and forks and crockery used in refreshment rooms and dining cars."

Betjeman goes on to talk about some of the individual styles of each company "The Midland favoured Gothic, and so in a less expensive way did the Great Eastern. Greek learning dominated the London and North Western. The Great Northern went in for a reliable homeliness rather than beauty."

The difference in personality and culture between the Midland and the Great Northern is exemplified in their two London termini. The Midland Railway's St Pancras station is one of the finest and most extravagant Victorian Gothic buildings in the world. The fantastical hotel which fronts it, designed by Sir George Gilbert Scott and opened in 1873 – "a glorious piece of pompous window dressing"[2] was and may once again become, when the Channel Tunnel rail link finally arrives in St Pancras, one of the most luxurious in Europe, while Barlow's engine shed which lies behind the station was, when it was completed in 1876, the largest station roof in the world without internal supports. Everything the Midland Railway did in its prime was lush, extravagant and luxurious. Even its trains were designed for comfort, rather than speed.

The Great Northern on the other hand was "noted more for its trains than its buildings"[3] and its terminus was at Kings Cross right next door to St Pancras. Lewis Cubitt designed and his company constructed a functional, workmanlike structure, which was completed on time and within budget in 1852. "A superb architectural statement in its monumental plainness"[4], it could not be more different from St Pancras, its neighbour and erstwhile competitor.

Every railway company had its complement of designers, graphic artists, engineers and architects; sometimes they worked together, more often independently. Collectively their output was massive and longlasting. After the railway companies initiated these vast design programmes they were followed by shipping companies, department stores and other large and complex enterprises which needed a visual expression of coherence, discipline, hierarchy and precedence.

Some of the most interesting and important manifestations of this relatively early stage of environmental brand development had a powerful social purpose. Many of the individuals who ran the few great organisations which patronised design were pioneers with what we call today a strong sense of corporate social responsibility. They wanted their staff to live and work in pleasant, well designed environments. They wanted their customers to buy high quality, good looking products. Many of these companies built housing estates, model villages and towns for their workforce. Krupp at Essen in Germany and Cadbury at Bourneville in England were especially well designed

Companies such as AEG wanted to create what was called in the idiom of the time "the most intimate union between art and industry." Allgemeine Elektrizitäts Gesellschaft was established by Emil Rathenau in the early 1880s. Within twenty-five years it had become one of Germany's largest companies in the electrical field making hundreds of products from turbines to kettles. In 1907 Emil Rathenau and his son Walther commissioned Peter Behrens, a famous architect and designer, to be their artistic director. The appointment was announced not in the business pages but in the art column of the 28 July 1907 edition of the Berliner Tagesblatt. On 29 August 1907 Behrens published a piece called Kunst der Technik (Art in Industry) in which he described his vision at length. Put briefly it was to improve public taste. Between 1907 and 1914 Behrens and his team were commissioned to redesign buildings, products and communications material including the corporate symbol for AEG. Some of the buildings constructed by the team, notably the Turbine Hall in Berlin, were masterpieces both of modern architecture and corporate design. Behrens' associates on this vast programme included Walter Gropius, Adolf Meyer, Ludwig Mies van der Rohe and Le Corbusier, all of whom later became famous architects in their own right. The extraordinary collaboration between AEG and some of the greatest design talent of the twentieth century[5] fell to bits in 1914, at the outbreak of the First World War and was unhappily never revived, but its influence was very powerful and in some ways still resonates to this day.

AEG carried through one of the greatest commercial design and branding programmes the world has seen and it inspired a number of other organisations. In many European countries a small but influential group of enlightened companies commissioned designers and architects to create what we would now call branding or identity programmes.

In the 1930s Frank Pick made London Transport into the world's most sophisticated, beautiful, modern and civilised transport system, by using the best architects and designers he could find to create an integrated, easy to use London Transport.

Looking at the pitiful shambles that it has become it seems almost impossible to believe that London once led the world's great cities in the design and implementation of a big city transport system, but it is so. And vestigial remnants of this Golden Age can be seen to this day.

In Italy Camillo Olivetti and his son Adriano commissioned a design programme that was in place right up to the 1980s. Ettore Sottsass and Mario Bellini were just two of the great design consultants retained to project the Olivetti brand by the Olivetti company, whose policy had huge influence on design in Italy. Sibylle Kueherer[6] makes clear that Adriano Olivetti used design for social purposes. The company took great pride in the achievements of its architects and designers and celebrated their influence and significance on the Italian world.

This tradition of benevolence and social responsibility in environments and architecture remains alive and well although it competes within the corporate soul with other more commercially orientated influences.

Volkswagen AG based in the unlovely company town of Wolfsburg has done a lot through corporate environments and architecture to cheer it up. VW now understands that everything it does has to be coherently and powerfully branded. It

has opened Autostadt, a theme park "for all those who love driving"(sic) outside Wolfsburg. Autostadt describes itself in a press release as "a brand-new type of automotive theme world and center (sic) of excellence", a "global forum of auto-mobility". In this "automobile city the general perspective of Volkswagen Group and the unique identity of each of its brands will become tangible in an inspiring atmosphere of creativity, individuality and dynamism."

The VW press release goes on to say "The brand pavilions are located in a park criss-crossed by waterways. In their architecture alone, each is a statement of the respective brand philosophy drawing the visitor into its interior – the stage in a brand temple." "They [the pavilions] are designed to allow visitors to walk through and experience with their own senses the thoughts, dreams, wishes and visions of the individual Volkswagen group brands."

In addition VW has opened a new assembly plant in Dresden. It is the most beautiful car plant in the world, though that's not necessarily much of a challenge. The flagship VW Phaeton is to be assembled at the Dresden factory where customers will be welcome to watch their cars being put together.

All these efforts from VW are in some senses reminiscent of the most complex and sophisticated employer of branded environments and architecture in the corporate world today – Disney.

Disney is a phenomenon. There is much about Disney that many people dislike. The corporation is said to be ruthless. It overpays its bosses. Some even say it is losing its grip. But if you went to any Disneyland or Disney World anywhere you certainly wouldn't know that. Disney has created a world of interrelated brands all based around a not very good drawing of a mouse said to have been created by the sainted Walt Disney himself in the mid 1920s. The Disney brand proliferates. Every time there's a new Disney movie, there are a whole bunch of new Disney brands.

Some of the brands like Snow White and the Seven Dwarfs and Dumbo are around 6o years old or more. But they are still pretty sprightly.

Disney has an amazing distribution system. There's the movie, the book, the rest of the merchandising, the TV channel, the musical, the Ice show and above all the three dimensional environmental/architectural apotheosis of the brand – the Theme Park.

The Theme Park is where all the bits come together. You can stroll down Main Street with your kids and they can meet Mickey or Goofy and with a bit of luck they can get to hold his hand. They can go on Disney rides, buy Disney memorabilia, stay in Disney hotels. They are surrounded, virtually engulfed by Disney. This is corporate branding at its most excessive, seductive and successful. You may not like it much, but it works. There is Disney's Epcot in Florida, a whole world full of different but disturbingly Disney environments.

Above all there's Celebration, a Disney town where every house is a dream house, where all the gardens are beautiful, where all the garbage disappears without a trace, where only the happy clappy live. And, this is the strange bit, in Celebration you have to buy your home like every other family anywhere. Some people genuinely choose of their own free will, to live in this Disney branded town.

And just ask yourself, in its gargantuan size, its power to overwhelm, its overweening self-confidence, its arcane and to some mysterious languages, rituals and customs and above all in its self worship and the deification of its founder, how different is a Disney Theme Park from the pyramids?

Corporate architecture hasn't changed all that much in 4,500 years.

Wally Olins
London, 2003

*Wally Olins is a co-founder of Wolff Olins and was chairman of the company until 1998. He is Chairman of Saffron Brand Consultants.

He has advised many of the world's leading organisations on identity, branding, communication and related matters. He has worked in the public sector with the Metropolitan Police, the National Housing Federation and many other bodies. He has worked with a number of countries on branding issues. He has also acted as advisor both to McKinsey and Bain on branding and marketing.

He is one of the world's most experienced practitioners of corporate identity and branding. His main interests are the big ideas behind organisations, and mergers and acquisitions. He has a particular interest in and experience of the branding of regions and nations.

1) Sir John Betjeman, London's Historic Railway Stations, John Murray, London 1972
2) David Atwell's chapter in Railway Architecture, ed. Marcus Binney and David Pearce, Orbis Books, London 1979
3) Sir John Betjeman – as before
4) David Atwell – as before
5) Tilmann Buddensieg and Henning Rogge, Industriekultur: Peter Behrens and the AEG, 1907 – 1914, MIT Press, Cambridge MA, 1984
6) Sibylle Kueherer, Olivetti: A Study of the Corporate Management of Design, Rizzoli, New York, 1990

in accordance with table 302.1.1 or the building shall be classified as a mixed occupan-

in each story, the building area shall be such that the sum of the ratios of the floor area of each use divided by the allowable area for each use shall n-

factory industrial group f occupancy includes, among others, the use of a building or structure, or a portion thereof, for assembling, disassembling, fabricating, finishing, manufacturing, packaging, repair or processing operations that are not classified as a group h hazardous or group s storage occupancy.

and 2. has a boiling point of 68° f(20° c) or less at 14.7 psi (101 kpa) which is either liquefied, nonliquefied or in solution, exce-

those gases which have no other health- or physical- hazard properties are not considered to be compressed until the pressure in the packaging exceeds 41 psi (282 kpa) at 68° f(20° c).

division 1.6. extremely insensitive articles which do not have a mass explosion hazard.

1. is ignitable at 14.7 psi (101 kpa) when in a mixture of 13 percent or less by volume with air; or 2. ha-

flammable range at 14.7 psi (101 kpa) with air of at least 12 percent, regardless of the lower limit.

20

100percentshopping

Retail Heaven – Retail Hell?
The Design Challenge of the New Consumers

Few areas of human activity can, at least outwardly, have altered as little over the ages as has retailing. Phoenician physicians, scientists, boat builders or farmers transported by a time machine from 2500 BC to the present century would be utterly baffled by the complexities of modern medicine, technology, shipyards, and agriculture. Yet Phoenician shop keepers dropped into almost any present day retail premises would find themselves in largely familiar surroundings with shelves on which goods are displayed, counters on which they are examined and scales on which they are weighed.

There are good reasons for supposing, however, that despite continuing largely unchanged for millennia, these familiar features of retailing are destined to alter out of all recognition within the next few decades. Computer technology combined with the changing demands and desires of modern consumers are creating forces that will transform the nature of retailing and, with it, the design of retail premises for ever. Far from continuing, as in the past, to be essentially "warehouses" for storing and displaying merchandise retail outlets will, through their design and construction, come to play a crucial role in gaining and retaining the loyalty of consumers.

Rather than forming a passive environment in which purchases are made, they will increasingly form a vital part of the marketing message by retailers seeking to communicate their unique differences to consumers. Le Corbusier's famous dictum that: "Une maison est une machine-à-habiter" (A house is a machine for living in) will have to be restated as "retail premises are machines for marketing."

To see why this is so, it will be useful briefly to consider the history of retailing and to track the emergence of a new breed of consumers.

A Brief History of Retailing
The historical processes leading to contemporary patterns of consumption in Europe and North America have been in existence for less than two centuries.

Before 1850, economies on both continents were primarily agricultural and populations predominantly rural.

This type of society offers only three main ways of buying finished consumer goods:

(1) Trade shops linked to particular craft guilds, such as grocers, haberdashers, and various kinds of mercers.
(2) Retailers who are also manufacturers, e.g. blacksmiths, and cabinet makers.
(3) Markets and occasional fairs at which agricultural products grown locally could be bought alongside imported items provided by itinerant traders, peddlers and bagmen who carried with them whatever they thought might be saleable.

"The system, however Spartan compared with today's retailing system, was already a development on practices common before 1800 which emphasised self-sufficiency and the use of fairs and periodic markets," comment Larry O'Brien and Frank Harris in their book Retailing: Shopping, Society, Space.

The early decades of the 19th century saw a population movement in the UK from rural to urban living. By around 1850, however, more people lived in towns and cities than in the countryside, with a consequent reduction in self-sufficiency and an increasing dependence on manufactured items for day-to-day survival. A rising and increasingly urban population, buoyant economy and low unemployment created demands for new goods and services. These, in turn, increased the rate of industrialisation, encouraging the development of new methods of mass production and mass transportation.

In little more than a century (see Table One) individuals had been transformed from active participants in the production of items for their own use to passive consumers of virtually everything.

Table 1.

Predominant Economy	Contribution made by consumer	Contribution made for consumer
Agricultural Up to 18th century	75%	25%
Industrial 1850 – 1960	25%	75%
Proto-Information Era 1960 – Early 1990s	40%	60%
Information Era: Early 1990s – 2050	50%	50%

The start of the 'sixties saw a shift to a different sort of economy in the West, an economy where information became the main resource of production as jobs in "knowledge-management" and services began to outnumber blue-collar jobs for the first time.

As information was applied in an organised way to improve production, consumers were presented with improvements in choice and quality year upon year. As a result, since the early 'eighties, the pendulum has been swinging back again with the gradual emergence of what I termed, in a recent book[1] New Consumers.

Even more recently a further sub-group has emerged within these rapidly expanding New Consumers, those who desire an even more active involvement in many aspects of production and whom Alvin Toffler has appropriately termed Prosumers.

Old Consumers, New Consumers and Prosumers
The terms "Old" and "New" do not refer to chronological age but to attitudes towards consumption. New Consumers transcend all boundaries of gender, ethnic origin, religion, income and age. You can find them among some of the lowest earners in the land and among the wealthiest. They inhabit classrooms, offices, boardrooms and retirement homes.

The forces shaping the attitudes of "Old Consumers" are those of mass marketing, mass production and mass consumption. As a result Old Consumers tend to be cautious, passive and reactive in their consumption. They feel safest when purchasing goods and services identical to those of their immediate neighbours and dislike anything too novel, too unfamiliar or too original. Their loyalty can be won by delivering reasonable quality at competitive prices.

Much of their consumption is also founded in well-established habits and satisfactions. If they have always bought Product X which can be picked up easily and conveniently at the local supermarket and costs less than Product Y, which can only be tracked down in small, specialist shops, they can see no good reason to change.

Even if Product Y was demonstrably more effective or efficient, it would take a great deal of persuasion to cause Old Consumers to make the switch. This is not to deny that economic necessity plays a role in many purchasing decisions, for both New and Old Consumers. But cost alone is by no means always the major consideration. Even when there is no difference in price, or they could easily afford the extra cost, Old Consumers locked into traditional patterns of purchase are far less likely to change their buying habits than are New ones. So far as they are concerned, if plastic costs half as much and lasts twice as long as wood, why waste time and money on timber?

The attitudes of New Consumers, by contrast, are shaped by recognition of a world in which a majority of the world's industries produce far more goods than customers are able to purchase resulting in an overcapacity that has led to hyper-competition and margin-slashing price wars. Raised in a media-saturated culture, where images are all powerful they are more visually literate than any group of consumers before them. Their lifestyles are dominated by high expectations, a demand for instant gratification and a passion for novelty. Their span of both attention and desire are shorter than at any time in the history of marketing. As a result they look on reliability and competitive prices as their "right" rather than something they should feel grateful for receiving.

Merely providing what the Japanese call "atarimae hinshitsu" or the "quality that is expected" will not be sufficient to ensure their loyalty. This can only be gained by consistently delivering "miryokuteki hinshitsu" or a "quality that fascinates."

Authenticity and the New Consumer
Whereas the goal for many Old Consumers was the accumulation of material possessions, the imperative for New Consumers is to self-actualise: that is to develop creatively, intellectually and spiritually as well as materially. This has led to a quest for what is special and authentic, in order to make themselves feel more special, more individual and, in a sense more "authentic." It is this search for the real as opposed to the artificial, for the original rather than the replica and the natural in favour of the synthetic that underlies much of their consumption.

New Consumers are more likely to seek out items which are different, and in some ways special. Because wood is natural, and therefore "authentic," it is their preferred material for a wide range of both the products they buy and the surroundings in which they make those purchases.

Searching for authenticity – in everything from food to fashions and foreign holidays to furniture – obliges New Consumers to be active rather than passive. It requires them to hunt down the individualised product and service while rejecting, so far as is possible, the standardised.

It compels them to act independently rather than swimming with the tide of product "synchronised" Old Consumers.

In a world where the "authenticity" of many products is becoming ever more central to their success the building design itself must communicate a sense of authenticity and integrity.

The Growing Power of Prosumers
Within this group of New Consumers there has, more recently, emerged the new sub-group of Prosumers to which I referred earlier. These use their own input into the production process to satisfy their desire for speed, to enable them to trust the final product (after all whom can they trust if not themselves) and to feel their eventual purchase is somehow more authentic because a part of them is a part of that product or service. Although a minority at present it seems likely that, in many areas of retailing, Prosumers will make an increasingly significant impact of the market over the next few years. These areas will include:

Food sales: Rather than offering pre-packaged meals, food retailers will increasingly prepare dishes based on an individual Prosumer's dietary preferences. Either on line, through text messaging or in person, Prosumers will be able to specify the ingredients used, how they are cooked, the ways in which they would like them presented and when they want to collect them.

Clothes sales: Prosumers, aided by computers, will be able to design their own fashions, try out different styles in cyberspace and have them delivered to their homes a few hours later.

Music sales: The global music market is predicted to rise significantly over the next few years, with sales of $47.5 billion being achieved within the next twelve months. This will be due to increased use of computers and digital delivery systems introduced by record companies which will enable consumers to compile their own CDs, mini-disc or MP3 files containing only those tracks by their favourite artist - or artists - they specifically want to hear. "It's…the first step toward separating music content from the delivery medium," says technology writer Richard Dean: "In a world of unlimited bandwidth, music labels have less to offer. It's this shift the recording industry fears."

Car sales: The motor showrooms of tomorrow will possess few if any actual models. Using video walls, computer screens, and holographic images, prospective purchasers will be able to design their own ideal vehicle, specifying everything from engine size and exterior colour to interior lay out and trim.

The ability of manufacturers to collaborate in this way with Prosumers is due to three advances in information technology.

First is the expansion of consumer databases, which enable producers to treat them as individuals. Second is the interactivity, which enables consumers to communicate easily and directly both with producers and with one another. Finally, and deriving directly from the above, there is the ability to "mass customise" products and services as a matter of routine. While, not so long ago, production lines were set up to produce millions of identical items, these days it is technically possible, at least with certain types of merchandise, to have a production line of one. Combining these three capabilities creates a "customer feedback loop" carrying the comforting message: "I know you and I remember you. Tell me what you want and I will make it for you." The challenge to designers and architects, therefore, is to find the means for embodying and satisfying these demands within retail premises. Before considering how this might be accomplished, however, we need to draw a distinction between two forms of shopping and two very different types of motivation and behaviour.

Doing the Shopping vs. Going Shopping
"Doing the shopping" involves buying such unexciting domestic necessities as detergent, bleach, dog or cat food and paper towels. Even the most dedicated shopper derives little or no pleasure from such activities, their desire being only to get a disagreeable and time consuming task over and done with in the shortest possible time.
Increasingly this chore is being relegated to Internet purchases; a trend which I believe will increase significantly over the next decade.

The task of designers creating retail premises for "doing the shopping" is to find ways of enabling large numbers of people to move into, through, and out of these commodity "warehouses" as speedily, efficiently and effortlessly as possible. This is, of course, no simple task and one which demands considerable psychological and technological insight. The work of American retailing anthropologist Paco Underhill,

for example, has demonstrated the importance of including what he terms a "decompression zone" between the entrance and the first shelves. This buffer zone in which no goods are displayed enables newly arriving shoppers to slow down their pace from pavement walking speed to shelf "browsing" speed, as well as to adjust physiologically to the differences in light levels, ambient temperature and so forth.

Technological innovations have enabled some stores to speed progress through the "cash and wrap" process by enabling customers to by-pass check out queues by using a personal bar-code reader to scan in their purchases and total the cost. This can then be paid by swiping a card through the reader before walking straight out of the store. New Consumers love the speed and "individual" feel to the service this technology provides, and feel no resentment at working as unpaid cashiers.
So far as they are concerned, speed and convenience fully recompenses for any inconvenience Involved.

While "doing the shopping," is an activity that is both planned and time limited, "going shopping," is usually open ended and lacks any precise plans or destinations. For many people it has become a leisure activity, the source of profound pleasure and excitement, which is separate from any purchases made. It is in this activity that, I believe, the importance of design is likely to become paramount.

The needs of someone "doing the shopping" tend to be fairly unambiguous and satisfying them will, among other things, depend on designing premises in which the required item can be rapidly found and easily purchased.

Although someone "going shopping" may not have any specific purchase need in mind when leaving home he or she will hope to be entertained, surprised and delighted as much by the process of consumption as by any products that are ultimately purchased. In pursuit of these goals our fickle, demanding, informed and impatient New Consumer or Prosumer will be far more attracted by retail premises which best satisfy their emotional rather than merely their physical demands.
It is here that the role of the designer in creating a structure capable of communicating all these "pleasure and leisure" benefits becomes of prime importance.

While a "warehouse" retail premises in which produce is "piled high and sold cheap" may generally satisfy the demands of many of those "doing the shopping" it will not come even close to matching the desires of someone "going shopping."

Back to the Future
In meeting these desires designers will, in a sense, be stepping back into the early history of department stores which, in their hey-day, were far more than places where merchandise was bought and sold. During the 19th century they formed just one part of the vast expansion of spectacular public space, which included great international exhibitions, galleries, leisure gardens, museums and, sometime later, the cinema, which offered an astonishing range of facilities, entertainments and visual pleasures.

These "monuments to modernity," as a contemporary writer described them, were visited as much for the interest and pleasure they provided in themselves as for the products they sold and services they supplied. They were true "fantasy palaces," designed in the most luxurious styles and purpose built using both modern and traditional materials. Their interiors often included grand open staircases and galleries, ornate iron work, domed glass roofs, walls covered in marble or mirrors, parquet floors covered with Eastern carpets. Department stores were among the earliest public buildings to be centrally heated and use electric light for both illumination and dramatic effect.

Drawing on the conventions of the theatre when displaying their merchandise and in their use of colour, they strove to create constantly new, vivid and seductive environments. In France the new photographic techniques were used to create an illusion of travelling not only in exotic places but also by balloon above the sea and to the surface of the Moon.

As well as all these visual delights major department stores offered customers a range of facilities designed to enhance their convenience, comfort and pleasure when "going shopping." These often included supervised children's areas, a library, art gallery, bank, ticket and travel agency, hairdressing salon, writing room, restaurants and roof top gardens – in some cases complete with pergolas, zoos and ice rinks!

"Visiting the stores during this period became, then, an excursion, an exciting adventure in the phantasmagoria of the urban landscape," says writer Mica Nava.[2]

Sadly, the same cannot be said of the vast majority of shopping experience today. Congested aisles, poorly displayed and hard to find goods, noise, heat and inadequately trained staff all contained with visually depressing surroundings, frequently transforms what was once a process of ecstatic exploration and discovery into a stressful, disagreeable and time consuming ordeal.
To succeed in gaining and retaining the attention, interest and loyalty of New Consumers and Prosumers, then, designers must somehow create spaces which – while not attempting slavishly to copy or recreate past glories somehow manage to modernise and encapsulate the same feelings of awe, thrill and delight known to our 19th century ancestors.

These then are the challenges which designers - and their retail clients - face over the coming years. Challenged by the growing popularity, ease and convenience of Internet shopping, they must find a way to rekindle the pleasures of shopping that so thrilled and delighted earlier generations.
At the same time, in order to cater for time conscious New Consumers and the desires of the Prosumers to play a more active role in the production of many products ways must be found of designing retail environments which satisfy both the demands of those shoppers who want to make their purchases at speed with those seeking a pleasurable shopping experience.
This is clearly no small challenge. Yet unless it is one that designers can surmount, both retailers and their customers face a future in which the possibility of creating retail heaven is increasingly overtaken by the reality of retail hell.

*David Lewis
Sussex, 2003

*David Lewis is a psychologist, international corporate speaker, best selling author and Chairman of the David Lewis Consultancy based in Southern England. He has been researching consumer behaviour for two decades. His most recent book is Soul of the New Consumer: Authenticity – What We Buy and Why in the New Economy.

[1] David Lewis and Darren Bridger (2001) Die Neuen Konsumenten: Was sie kaufen; Warum sie kaufen; Wie man sie als Kunden gewinnt . Frankfurt/New York Campus:Verlag
[2] Cited in Mica Nava Modernity's Disavowal, in: The Shopping Experience Eds. Pasi Falk & Colin Campbell

when	2001
where	castagnito – italy
client	rewe – billa italia
altitude above sea level	350.05 m
coordinates	44° 45' n 08° 02' e
weight/shop	6122.45 tons
total payload/shop	2813.20 tons
capacity/shop	1235 persons
construction time/shop	2144h23min
security options	middle
graphic design	section.d

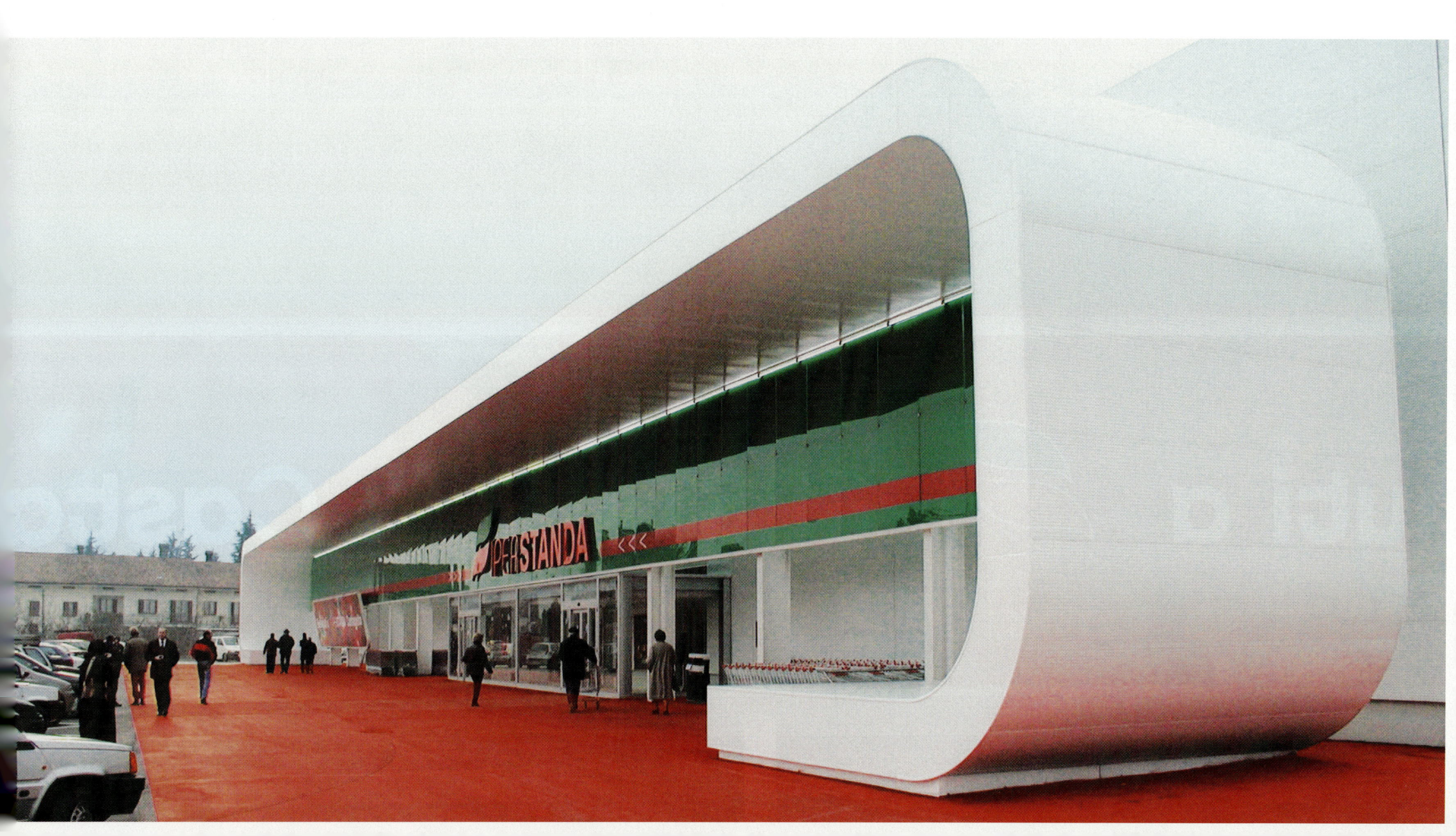

when	2000 - 2001
where	austria
client	telekom austria ag
quantity	12
altitude above sea level	117.30 – 724.90 m
coordinates	47° 20' n 13° 20' e
weight/shop	634.40 tons
total payload/shop	145.20 tons
capacity/shop	70 persons
construction time	339h55min
security options	high

jet2web

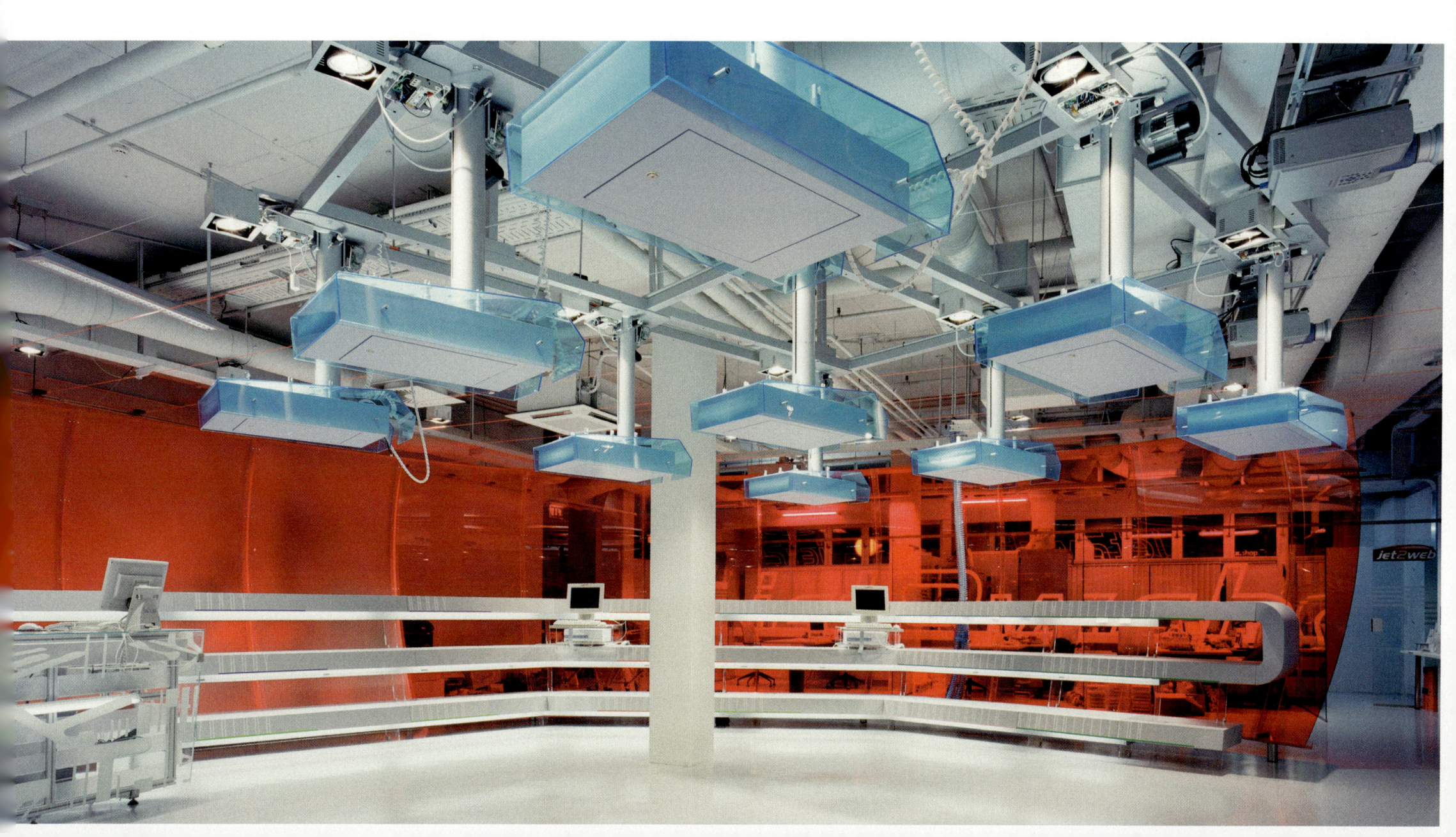

when	2001
where	leopoldsdorf – austria
client	rewe – merkur warenhandels ag
altitude above sea level	190.10 m
coordinates	48° 06' n 16° 23' e
weight/shop	3522.70 tons
total payload/shop	3005.10 tons
capacity/shop	860 persons
construction time	2642h15min
security options	middle

when	1999 - 2002
where	austria
client	mobilkom austria ag
quantity	45
altitude above sea level	117.30 – 724.90 m
coordinates	47° 20' n 13° 20' e
weight/shop	321.50 tons
total payload/shop	77.20 tons
capacity/shop	35 persons
construction time	336h25min
security options	middle

mobilkom

when	2003
where	all over austria
client	österreichische post ag
quantity	20
altitude above sea level	117.40 – 2020.15 m
coordinates	47° 20' n 13° 20' e
weight/shop	423.30 tons
total payload/shop	196.50 tons
capacity/shop	110 persons
construction time/shop	456h32min
security options	high
graphic design	section.d

shop

when	2001
where	vienna – austria
client	fonds & co ag
quantity	1
altitude above sea level	171.20 m
coordinates	48° 15′ n 16° 25′ e
weight/shop	1323.80 tons
total payload/shop	203.20 tons
capacity/shop	120 persons
construction time	971h35min
security options	high

when	1993
where	deutsch wagram – austria
client	rewe – merkur warenhandels ag
altitude above sea level	159.20 m
coordinates	48° 17' n 16° 34' e
weight/shop	5260.30 tons
total payload/shop	3872.30 tons
capacity/shop	920 persons
construction time	2712h45min
security options	middle
artist (sculpture)	irena rosc

merkur D

merkur D

when	1997
where	vienna – austria
client	palmers ag
quantity	1
altitude above sea level	174.90 m
coordinates	48° 15' n 16° 25' e
weight/shop	1192.30 tons
total payload/shop	173.50 tons
capacity/shop	85 persons
construction time	952h37min
security options	middle

palmers

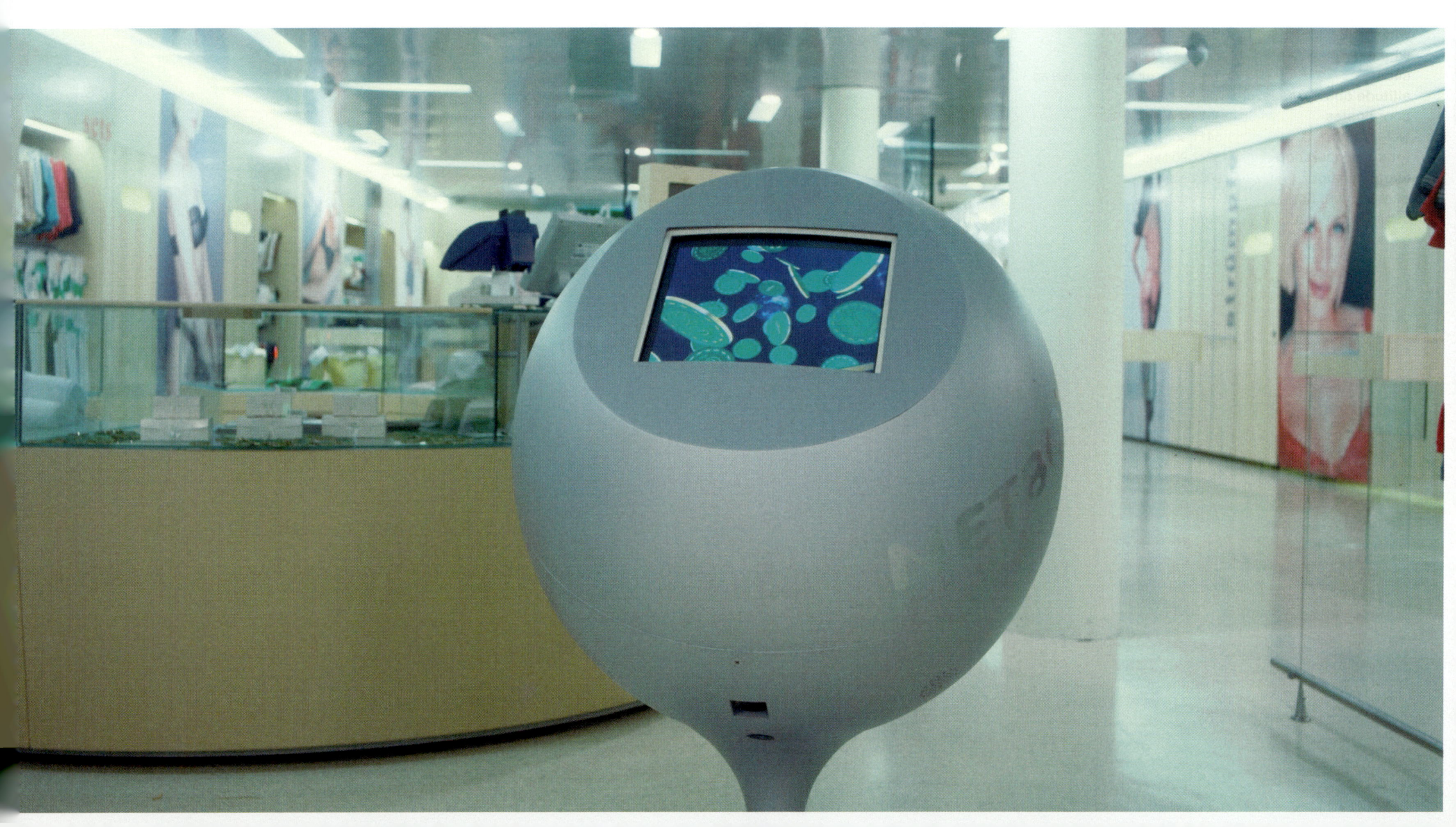

when	1999
where	vienna – austria
client	rewe – merkur warenhandels ag
altitude above sea level	222.90 m
coordinates	48° 15' n 16° 25' e
weight/shop	5411.30 tons
total payload/shop	3242.90 tons
capacity/shop	980 persons
construction time	2651h52min
security options	middle

when	1995
where	vienna – austria
client	wolford ag
quantity	1
altitude above sea level	171.80 m
coordinates	48° 15' n 16° 25' e
weight/shop	1285.30 tons
total payload/shop	244.50 tons
capacity/shop	90 persons
construction time	1656h09min
security options	middle

when	1995
where	vöcklabruck – austria
client	rewe – billa ag
quantity	1
altitude above sea level	440.25 m
coordinates	48° 00' n 13° 39' e
weight/shop	1042.65 tons
total payload/shop	623.20 tons
capacity/shop	310 persons
construction time	1562h12min
security options	middle

when	2002
where	graz – austria
client	rewe – merkur warenhandels ag
quantity	1
altitude above sea level	345.25 m
coordinates	47° 00' n 15° 23' e
weight/shop	7923.10 tons
total payload/shop	6624.30 tons
capacity/shop	2350 persons
construction time	2160h44min
security options	middle

when	1996-2003
where	all over austria
client	rewe – bipa parfumerien gesmbh
quantity	365
altitude above sea level	117.10 – 724.65 m
coordinates	47° 20' n 13° 20' e
weight/shop	841.35 tons
total payload/shop	203.90 tons
capacity/shop	120 persons
construction time	361h18min
security options	middle

bipa

when	1999-2003
where	all over austria
client	rewe – bipa parfumerien gesmbh / billa ag – sec. mondo
quantity	14
altitude above sea level	176.30 – 561.40 m
coordinates	47° 20' n 13° 20' e
weight/shop	1827.25 tons
total payload/shop	842.50 tons
capacity/shop	360 persons
construction time	1512h07min
security options	middle

synergy bipa/mondo

when	2001
where	vienna – austria
client	o & k restaurant betriebsges.m.b.h.
quantity	1
altitude above sea level	171.60 m
coordinates	48° 15' n 16° 25' e
weight	68.30 tons
total payload	4.75 tons
capacity	4 persons
construction time	324h41min
security options	middle

restroom o & k

each part of a building included within the exterior walls or the exterior walls and fire walls where provided shall be permitted to be a separate building.

1. mezzanines or portions thereof are not required to be open to the room in which the mezzanines are located, provided that the occupant load of the aggregate area of t... enclosed space does not exceed

group- 2,h- 3 andh- 4 fire areas shall be permitted in unlimited area buildings having occupancies in groups f and s, in accordance with the limitations of this section.

1. the building above the horizontal assembly is not required to be of type i construction;

3. the height and the number of the floors above the basement shall be limited as specified in table 406.3.5.

1. more than 6 fee (1829 mm) above grade plane;

the height and area for buildings of different construction types shall be governed by the intended use of the building and shall not exceed the limits in table 503 except as modified hereafter.

88

100percentbanking

Trust me: Money's Bond Between Strangers

What is money? When asked, most people would respond with a physical description of specific coins or currency. But money is so much more than that. Economists describe it as a "store of value" having certain key properties. For one, it must be durable. Perishables such as grain or similar natural objects do not qualify. Money must be uniform and dividable into smaller quantities. Without uniformity, quantities of money could not be readily compared or exchanged. Without divisibility, the use of money would be limited to the wealthiest segments of society. If the only form of money were an object with a value of, say, a year's wages for a laborer, then it would be useless in everyday commerce.

Precious metals such as gold and silver exhibit these key attributes and have been used as stores of value for centuries. The metals are durable; when refined, they are completely uniform; and they can be divided into units of arbitrary size. But anyone accepting such metals in exchange for goods or a service has a problem – how to ascertain that indeed the metal is of the proper weight, composition and fineness. Well, a scale can be used to check the weight, and chemicals can be used to check the composition and fineness. In fact, these tools are exactly what merchants of old used in the daily transaction of business. As recently as the mid-19th century, such tools were still used in the American West: Miners brought grains and nuggets of gold and silver to town to purchase provisions.

Raw metals, however, fail the uniformity and divisibility tests. To properly function as money, they must be refined and divided into standard units. This is how coins first came into being centuries ago. The moneyer, having performed his service, would mark each finished coin with an inscription attesting to the weight and fineness of the piece. He would also include a symbol identifying himself as the moneyer. Those in the community who knew him and respected his integrity would accept his coins without question. The use of scales and chemicals was no longer essential in each exchange. And as coins traded hands with less scrutiny, commerce greatly speeded up.

This tremendous leap in commerce depended on an equally tremendous leap of faith by the general population – individuals placed their trust in the moneyer. They no longer verified his work: They recognized his mark and trusted that it represented full value. This placement of trust is the oil that has lubricated the machinery of world economies ever since. Every single advancement in the mechanisms of exchange and every financial instrument and institution created in the history of the world is built on this simple foundation of trust.

Coinage quickly developed into the form we readily recognize thousands of years later. The early moneyer's marks evolved into elaborate designs serving multiple purposes: Not only the most obvious, to identify the issuer (typically a monarch or government), but also to reflect a statement of weight, fineness or denomination. It became customary to include the year of issuance as well as a mint mark to identify the manufacturing facility. Together, these design elements identified the object as a store of a certain value. The design elements had a secondary goal – to discourage counterfeiting and other forms of cheating such as "clipping." Unscrupulous individuals sometimes cut or shaved small bits of precious metal from coins that passed through their hands, thus cheating the next recipient and gradually collecting a valuable amount of metal. Just as an elaborately engraved design foiled imitators, a design that filled the coin all the way to the edges curtailed the practice of clipping.

Paper money followed a similar development. One point of origin was with the silversmiths and goldsmiths who issued written receipts for the precious metals people left with them. Over time, the community's trust in the smiths made their paper receipts "as good as gold." People would trade the receipts without having to physically take possession of the metal. Thus, metalsmiths became the forerunners of modern bankers and their receipts, early forms of paper money. The key: people's trust in the issuer. Today that trust is complete: Our paper money is no longer backed by actual silver or gold; it is worth only what people agree it is worth.

The present-day use of money is so ingrained that people everywhere take it for granted, never questioning the assumptions that make it all work. Enter J.S.G. Boggs, an artist of our time whose work probes the fundamental nature of money and individual and societal relationships with it. His artwork can be viewed and appreciated in museums and private collections, but only a personal encounter with the artist brings out the full flavor of his work.

Connoisseurs need not apply – Boggs interacts with the common man. A typical encounter: Upon entering a store, Boggs picks up several items and takes them to the counter for the clerk to tally the total. Rather than paying with money of the realm, Boggs offers to exchange the goods for one of his artworks – a small drawing or print of his own design rendered in similar fashion to the appropriate paper money. Boggs makes no attempt to pass off his work as "real money." In fact, he volunteers to pay in legally valid currency if the clerk prefers. But the acceptance of Boggs' work acknowledges that the fruit of his labors represents some value to the world.

In most cases, the clerk's first impulse is to laugh or call the manager or police. But some consider what the artwork is "worth" and weigh the offer seriously. Many simply decline and ask for "real money." Once in a while, once in a very long while, someone will agree to accept the art, and, in deference to their employer, take the equivalent in "real money" from their wallet or purse and place it in the register. At this point, Boggs requests a receipt and change for the transaction. He wants his note to be accepted at exactly the face value of the real money, with change given in return, and a receipt to document the transaction.

Scenes like this have been played out in restaurants, hotel lobbies, taxicabs and drinking establishments worldwide. Time and again, Boggs is refused. He has not only been arrested on numerous occasions and prosecuted in England and Australia, but also his studio has been raided and his works confiscated by the U.S. Secret Service. He has, however, never been convicted of a crime. Dancing in the gray areas of the law, he presses on.

Boggs' mission is to make people think about something they take for granted: money. What is this stuff we use every day yet rarely pay any attention to? Physically, currency is just a piece of paper. But currency is also art, and a close examination of any piece of currency will reveal thousands of intricate details of design. A piece of currency can be thought of as a limited edition print. These objects are beautiful, yet their very familiarity lulls us into looking right past that attribute. The portrait of George Washington on the U.S. one dollar bill is based on a painting from life by Gilbert Stuart. It is probably the single most reproduced work of art in the history of the world. The U.S. government prints millions of them a day. But a bill hand-drawn by an artist such as Boggs is unique – one of a kind. Even a printed edition of 100 such unofficial notes is extremely rare in comparison to "real money." If the design is pleasing to the eye, if the concept is thought-provoking, if the work is rare or unique, then why shouldn't it be "worth" as much or more as the "real money"?

Collectors of Boggs' work have an answer to this question. They are eager to trade "real money" for an example of his work. Having completed a transaction, Boggs often contacts a collector who has expressed interest in his work. He sells the receipt and change to the collector (the artist has to make a living somehow …). The collector seeks out the clerk, the waiter or waitress, the taxi driver or the bartender who accepted the artwork and offers to pay several times face value for it. Sometimes, the transaction is made. Just as often, Boggs' original contact chooses to keep his artwork after having had their judgment of value reinforced by a stranger.

In its physical form, money is merely an object, albeit an often beautiful and overlooked object. It is what the object stands for that is most important. It represents trust – that faith we have in our fellow human beings to stick to their word and deliver on their promises.

MONEY IS TRUST. TRUST LUBRICATES THE MACHINERY OF FINANCE, AND WITHOUT IT, THE WORLD ECONOMY WOULD GRIND TO A HALT.

What is a bank? If you are like most people, you probably have money stored in several places: Your pockets may hold some coins; your wallet or purse may hold some paper money; you may also have money in a bank. At its most basic, a bank is a place where individuals and businesses store money. A bank is also a place where money can grow; depositors can earn interest in return for the use of their deposited funds. It is a clearinghouse for transfers of money between individuals, business and other financial institutions.

Money and other valuables can be stored physically in a bank's vault. Money can be deposited in various types of accounts, such as checking, savings or certificates of deposit. What makes a bank work is the same principle that makes money itself work – trust. Placing one's money in the hands of another person or institution is an act of faith. One simply trusts that the transaction is in good faith and that the trustee is honorable. A certificate of deposit is a mere symbol representing the money deposited, just as paper money itself is merely a symbol of value – and that symbol is paramount.

Robert Morris, the financier of the American Revolution, knew full well the importance of symbolism and imagery in building trust. As a founder of the Bank of North America, a forerunner of the U.S. Federal Reserve System, he knew there was an ever-present danger that investors would lose confidence and make a run on the bank, depleting its reserve of gold and silver coin. To help allay depositors' concerns, he placed reflectors around the cashier's cages, which magically multiplied the gleaming stacks of coins.

Reinforcing an image with mirrors is one thing, but using fake documents to cover up thievery is quite another. The slightest hint of legerdemain could devastate a banking institution, for it causes the very foundation of trust to crumble. Cases of bank fraud are relatively rare, but some are astounding in their audacity. One such case occurred in the town of New Berlin, New York, at the turn of the 20th century. Frank T. Arnold, cashier of the First National Bank of New Berlin, took over the reins upon the death of his friend and mentor John T. White. Arnold was well known and well respected, and the bank's board of directors never challenged his decisions. Many townspeople trusted him so much that they let him keep their personal stocks and bonds for safekeeping. Unfortunately, the town's trust was misplaced.

Arnold began to live extravagantly; he spread word of "an inheritance". With an annual salary of only $1,800, he purchased a $12,000 mansion and spent twice that sum remodeling and decorating it. Among his household employees, a cook, a butler and a coachman; among his possessions, a new $5,000 Packard automobile. Eventually, rumors about Arnold led worried depositors to withdraw $5,000 daily from the bank, and Arnold confessed to having looted the bank's coffers. For more than a decade, he had manipulated the books, fooled the auditors and abused the trust of the depositors. He even stole money from a local church's cemetery fund, donated it to the church for a new building and then stole it back again when the church re-deposited it. In all, he is believed to have looted $361,000 from a bank that had deposits of just $371,000. The bank collapsed; Arnold was convicted and sent to federal prison.

BANKS ARE BUILT ON A DELICATE FOUNDATION OF TRUST. WITHOUT IT, THEY CRUMBLE.

The crime of the (last) century occurred half a world away in Portugal. In 1924, 28-year-old amateur criminal and failing businessman Artur Virgilio Alves Reis sat down to plan the perfect crime. His plan was outrageous, flat-out crazy – but it was just crazy enough to work, almost. Although Reis was often laughably lax with detail, he had one principal tenet right. He understood to the bone that trust is key to the functioning of the entire economic system – thus, the most dangerous criminal is not an armed thug but a confidence man. The man who wins the trust of others can steal fortunes without firing a shot.

In Portugal, the national currency was issued by the Bank of Portugal, a private corporation with close connections to the government. The notes themselves were printed by the venerable London firm of Waterlow & Sons. Waterlow printed banknotes for most of the British colonies, the Bank of Scotland, Greece, Bolivia and Costa Rica as well as Portugal.

At the heart of Reis' scheme was counterfeiting, one of the oldest tricks in the criminal repertoire. But Reis would be no ordinary counterfeiter. He knew it was a losing game to attempt to duplicate modern notes expensively produced with the full resources of a government. No matter how close a copy is made, there is always some detail that will give it away. The only perfect copies of banknotes come from the original printing process. Reis' innovation was at once astoundingly bold and incredible in its simplicity. He counterfeited the papers authorizing the printing of notes by Waterlow on behalf of the Bank of Portugal. A well-connected accomplice of Reis traveled to London and presented Waterlow with official-looking credentials and letters accompanied by a plausible request for secrecy and expediency in processing the order. Although Waterlow followed up with several standard verification procedures, by either luck or design, no undue suspicions were raised. A shipment of $5 million worth of brand-new Portuguese 500 escudo notes was printed and delivered.

A man of modest means such as Reis spending piles of new notes would surely raise suspicions. Enlisting ne'er-do-wells to spend them wouldn't do either, for that would invite blackmailers and snitches. Such small plans were for small men – not Reis. Stage Two of his plan had already been sketched out. Reis became a respected businessman. In fact, he started a bank! By July 1925, the new Bank of Angola e Metropole was open for business. And a booming business it was. The new competitor came on strong, selling mortgages and undercutting established banks on loan and exchange rates. When depositors withdrew cash, more often than not they were given brand-new 500 escudo notes. The notes raised some suspicions, but when asked to authenticate the notes, the Bank of Portugal declared them genuine. Soon Reis was a wealthy man-about-town, living fashionably, his wife spending hundreds of thousands of dollars on jewelry, furs and gowns.

But Reis was not finished. Sooner or later, he realized, the truth could come out; he could be prosecuted for his crime. Reis knew Portuguese law well: Only the Bank of Portugal could initiate prosecution against counterfeiters. Enter Stage Three of his plan. Reis and his accomplices began using their profits to quietly acquire shares in the Bank of Portugal. By gaining majority control, Reis would guarantee that no one would prosecute. It was an absolutely brilliant plan, and it almost worked. Exactly one year after the appointment with Waterlow, the juggernaut stopped; banking competitors exposed his scheme. Reis, his wife and accomplices were arrested and their bank was closed.

In some cities there were serious runs on the Bank of Portugal, and mobs were dispersed by troops. Confidence in the country's currency was shattered. The public's faith in government was lost as well, enabling a military junta to take power in May 1926. Reis, like Arnold an ocean away, died in prison.

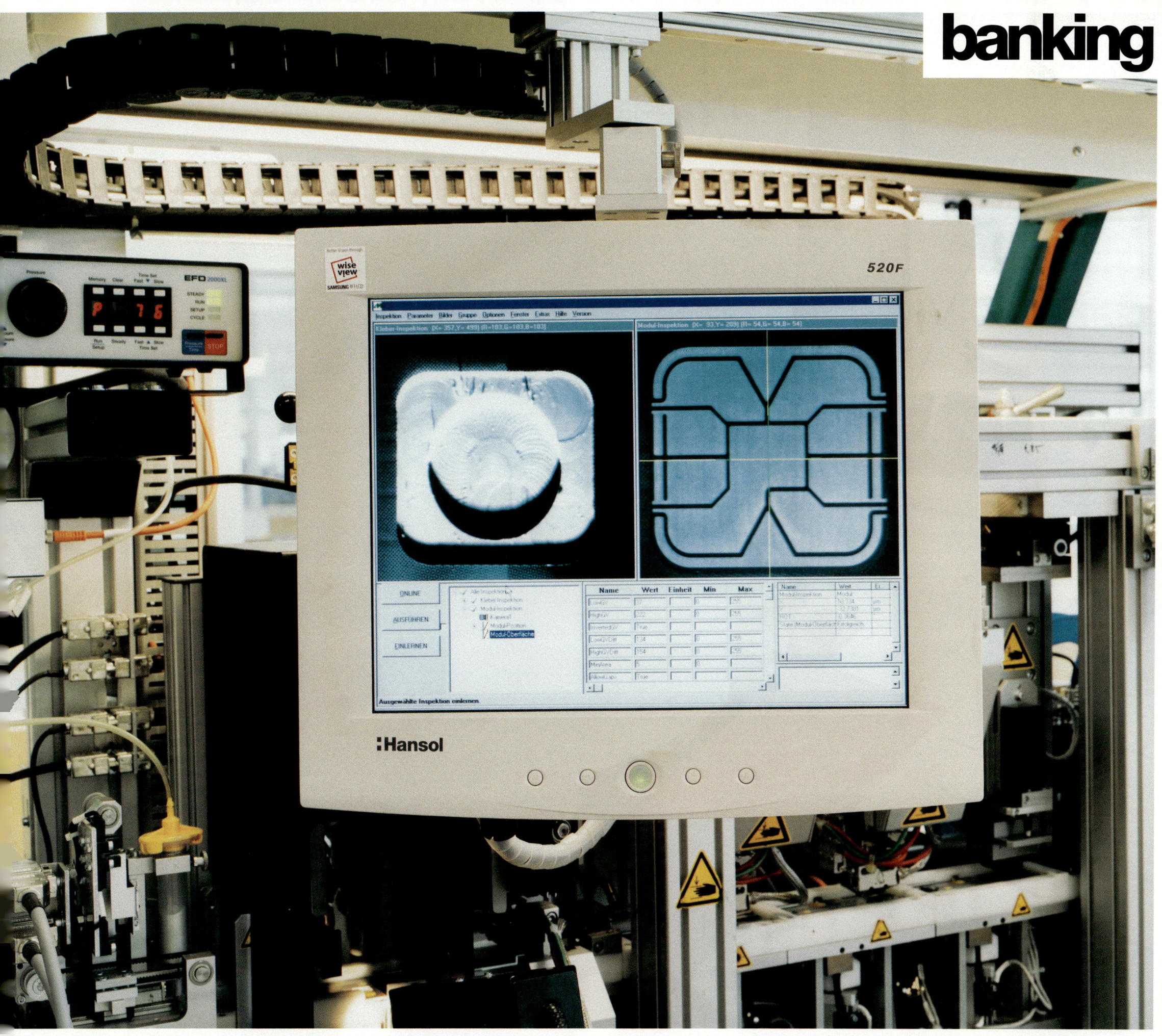

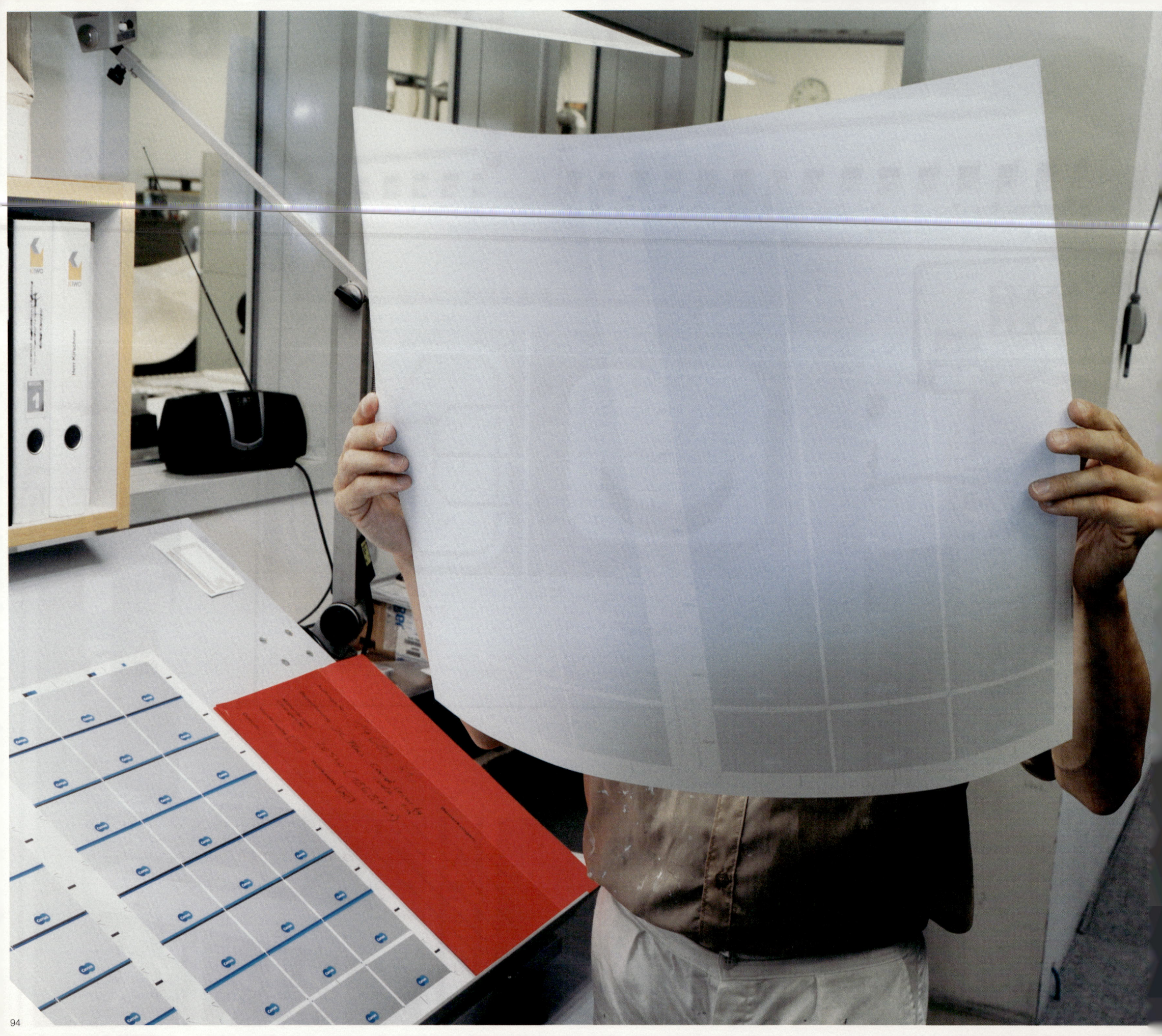

Arnold and Reis gained the trust of others. Their banks were trusted by their communities and became integral parts of the economy. When the violation of trust was revealed, the banks collapsed, and, in Reis' case, the collapse was so spectacular it brought an entire economy and government down with it.

What part does trust play today? The theme of trust in money, banking, business and the economy carries through to the modern world. Technology may change, but the underlying human condition does not. No matter what physical objects are involved, the central issue remains one of trust – that fragile yet powerful bond between strangers.

Before the advent of the automated teller machine (ATM), few would have dreamed that they would perform routine banking chores via a machine. Today, the machines are taken for granted because people have grown over time to trust them, the same way they grew to trust the human employees of their bank. Investing is also yielding to the electronic age. Not long ago, physical stock certificates were issued to represent ownership in a corporation. Gradually, people became comfortable with allowing intermediaries to hold their certificates, content to receive a summary report of their holdings and physical certificates became optional. Now, some corporations do not issue actual certificates under any circumstances. Ownership has become completely virtual.

Many of us do most of our banking and investing online, rarely dealing with a human being face-to-face or handling a physical stock certificate, paycheck or coin. Again, what once required a leap of faith is becoming commonplace. We are beginning to trust and embrace the digital world. Naturally, criminals have followed. One type of computer banking fraud involves an e-mail request of bank customers to click on a link that takes them to a fake Web site resembling the real one. Customers are asked for their account name and password, which the thieves use to ransack the real accounts. Fraud never goes away, it merely changes form.

Will bank buildings ever disappear? If we trust ATMs and Web sites with our banking transactions, do we need the bank building at all? Consider this, though: Would we still trust them if there were no longer any physical bank facilities affiliated with them? Experience shows the answer is clearly NO.

David S. Pottruck, president of discount broker Charles Schwab & Co., coined the phrase "clicks and bricks" to describe the melding of online and offline operations as a successful business model. He believes that virtual storefronts must complement and coexist with physical storefronts to harness the full power of the Internet – one without the other is incomplete. Schwab discovered this phenomenon serendipitously in the days before the Internet entered the mainstream.

Founded in 1974, the brokerage attracted clients who wanted to trade stocks without the high commission fees charged by other firms. Business was transacted by telephone and mail; branch offices were deemed an unnecessary expense. In 1975, Charles Schwab's uncle Bill Schwab wanted to invest $300,000 in the young company, but the money came with strings attached – he wanted the company to open a branch office in his hometown of Sacramento, California, and employ Bill's son-in-law as manager. After first resisting the notion, Charles gave in and opened his firm's first branch office.

The Sacramento public's response to the new office was astounding. The number of new accounts and amount of business in the city grew by leaps and bounds. The only explanation was that the physical branch mattered. The new office made the intangible tangible. Its mere presence tipped the psychological scales – people felt Schwab was a company they could trust with their money.

PHYSICAL PRESENCE IS A KEY COMPONENT OF TRUST IN BANKING.

Since physical bank buildings are here to stay, what form should they take? What are the essential elements? Can we define the key elements as concisely as economists defined the essential elements of money?

At its core, banking is about transactions between an individual and the bank. These transactions can take place in numerous ways, but nearly all are initiated by the customer, take place between the customer and an agent of the bank (human or mechanical) and are documented in some fashion for both parties. These core activities have taken place for thousands of years – a citizen of an urban center in the Middle Ages would have witnessed the same activities we see surrounded by modern trappings in banks today. These activities could take place on a street, in a bazaar, on the steps of a temple or in any manner of structure whatsoever. Bank structures can and do take a wide variety of forms.

In our crowded modern world, where individuals are unlikely to know one another personally, it is important that the physical surroundings reinforce the core element – trust. Banks must exude trust, and they can do this by projecting a businesslike appearance of solidity, stability, permanence, dignity, prestige and wealth.

THE ARCHITECTURE OF BANKS, EXCHANGES AND FINANCIAL BUSINESSES MUST EXUDE TRUST, PERMANENCE AND WEALTH. IMAGE IS PARAMOUNT.

It is no coincidence that the overriding features of a vast majority of bank facilities worldwide are designed to impart this appearance. Heavy stone walls, iron bars and vaults of steel and concrete are typical features, even in recent construction. Banks have a certain character that causes them to stand out in a community. Because of their central importance to society, they often occupy the most valuable real estate. Bank buildings are generally distinctive in their appearance, apart from their neighbors and instantly recognizable as financial institutions. Even the smallest banks endeavor to project through their facilities an image worthy of trust.

Central banks in urban centers are often the most elaborate, spacious, dramatic and powerful structures in town. In fact, with their soaring arches and classic columns some could easily be mistaken for churches. One such main bank branch in Pittsburgh, Pennsylvania, gained the nickname "The Cathedral of Earning" for its grand Greek Temple design. Bankers after all, have been called the high priests of finance. It is quite fitting for banks to echo ecclesiastical architecture, for what other structure is so implicitly trusted?

And what is trust if not faith? As discussed throughout this essay, the act of faith required to trust another person or institution is the bond that holds together the economy of the entire planet. Although often subtle, the architectural elements comprising a bank structure are critical components of the institution; they impart power. The physical form of a bank is inseparable from the institution; the image it projects is the primary factor in forming the crucial bond of trust in the mind of the customer. The physical form imparts an image, and the image is crucial.

THE DESIGN OF BANKING FACILITIES MUST CATER TO FUNDAMENTAL HUMAN NATURE. ALL ELEMENTS MUST DIRECTLY OR INDIRECTLY REINFORCE THE IMAGE OF TRUST.

Wayne K. Homren
Pittsburgh, 2003

*Wayne Homren is a financial analyst at Parker/Hunter, Inc. in Pittsburgh, PA, USA. He is a lifelong coin collector and Past President of the Numismatic Bibliomania Society. His collecting interests include money of the U.S. Civil War, numismatic literature, and the work of money artist J.S.G. Boggs.

when	1999
where	krems – austria
client	kremser sparkasse
quantity	1
altitude above sea level	201.70 m
coordinates	48° 24' n 15° 36' e
weight	1054.50 tons
total payload	175.2 tons
capacity	35 persons
construction time	1675h36min
security options	high

bank 4 you

when	1998
where	vienna – austria
client	creditanstalt investmentbank
quantity	1
altitude above sea level	171.80 m
coordinates	48° 15' n 16° 25' e
weight	1657.60 tons
total payload	721.35 tons
capacity	135 persons
construction time	1446h07min
security options	high

ca investmentbank

when	1999 - 2003
where	austria
client	österreichische verkehrskreditbank
quantity	3
altitude above sea level	175.40 – 367.50 m
coordinates	47° 20' n 13° 20' e
weight	63.80 tons
total payload	34.10 tons
capacity/shop	12 persons
construction time	501h17min
security options	high

verkehrskreditbank

ein unternehmen der BAWAG gruppe

verkehrskreditbank

verkehrskreditbank

when	1996
where	vienna – austria
client	girocredit bank ag
quantity	1
altitude above sea level	171.70 m
coordinates	48° 15' n 16° 25' e
weight	621.50 tons
total payload	123.30 tons
capacity	20 persons
construction time	1082h04min
security options	high

girocredit banking park

girocredit banking park

fixtures located within unisex toilet bathing rooms complying with section 404 of the international plumbing code are permitted to be included in determining the minimum required number of fixtures for assembly and mercantile occupancies.

1.1 unisex toilet and bath fixtures. fixtures located within unisex toilet bathing rooms complying with section 404 of the international plumbing code are permitted to be included in determining the minimum required number of fixtures for assembly and mercantile occupancies.

4. separate facilities shall not be required in mercantile occupancies in which the maximum occupant load is 50 or less.

exceptions: 1. separate facilities shall not be required for private facilities. 2. separate employee facilities shall not be required in occupancies in which 15 or fewer people are employed.

the required water closets, lavatories and showers or bathtubs shall be distributed equally between the sexes based on the percentage of each sex anticipated in the occupant load.

the provisions of this chapter and the international plumbing code shall govern the erection, installation, alteration, repairs, relocation, replacement, addition to, use or maintenance of plumbing equipment and systems.

100percentworking

Office Archaeology:
Anthropological and archaeological aspects of architecture and office work from a cultural and scientific perspective

Preamble
A short glance at the various aspects of observation is useful for an introductory exploration of the field of research. Afterwards, the attempt can be made to link the individual tendencies according to central themes. This can only be seen as a tenuous attempt at an analytical approach, since an extensive empirical research segment, which is required for a well-founded analysis, could not be completed for this study. For this reason, archaeological methodology was applied to observe the field of research, since it is based on source material that is constantly subject to rudimentary, selective mechanisms. This approach makes it possible to present one interpretation of reality based on the exposure and analysis of individual layers. At the same time, this implies that other conclusions are considered possible. However, much more is achieved than the proclamation of one truth when said approach or the aspects discussed succeed in engaging the reader's interest in the subject.

The Architecture Aspect
Architecture, which the Greeks considered the mother of all arts, and which was also rated one of the free arts during the Renaissance, satisfies the everyday need for a place to live, which is defined as one of the "soziale Totalphänomene" according to Marcel Mauss. The creation of architectures was established to address both living and working needs according to our understanding of Central European living space today. Its primary function with regard to a working environment lies in guaranteeing independence from the weather and organizing work procedures in a meaningful spatial program. Additionally, we tend to link secondary meanings to things and actions in our communication process-ridden, constitutionalized world. This aspect of immateriality has existed within the materiality of construction from the very beginning. One only has to think of "buildings" such as Stonehenge or the ancient Egyptian pyramids – the primary function is open to debate in one case. In the other case, the primary function as a tomb is clearly upstaged by the building's secondary function as a means of distinction and representation. The creation of architecture is a complex project in general terms – a bundle of demands, so to speak.

The Work Aspect
Diligence on the job has achieved a certain social recognition as a secondary virtue, especially in the German-speaking world. So, doesn't it make sense to stylize a work place and load it up with additional meanings? A short glance at the cultural history of office work makes the rapid transformation this field underwent in the course of – let us say – 120 years clear: from the workbench-like alignment of lecterns in the writing room or office cells lined up like a string of pearls with a "civil servant's track" running in between, to large open-space offices characterized by equal amounts of monitoring and distraction. Other examples include workflow-optimized work spaces with a PC and communications terminal with their adjustable wall panels that can be set to suit any work group configuration. Their efficiency is symbolized by the figures a cost-benefit calculation and the temporarily stationary sales representative who rolls his mobile office caddy to a non-personalized work space and logs into his virtual office via a network connection.

Every case also reflects society's esteem for office employees in its organization. Society's system of values undergoes a continuous transformation over time. The spectrum includes the criminal mastermind behind a desk in a public administration office and the investment banker, equipped with symbols of mobility such as a laptop and a mobile phone, although the latter only enjoyed a brief boom during the "new economy" months. What remains is a value system in which status defined by professional success, which is generally documented by the corresponding earnings, results in social recognition.

The Archaeology Aspect
Historically oriented cultural studies use different methods and types of sources to analyze and reconstruct historical processes. Archaeological methods are mainly based on the analysis of the remains of a culture's objects. A difference should be made between discoveries, the circumstances of the discovery and their contexts. The latter are particularly important since they allow conclusions on the former contexts of function and meaning – it is possible to unearth deeper meanings and patterns of action. Traces of use or indications of secondary uses also give interesting insights. Archaeology also avails itself of a number of generally natural science-based supplementary sciences that shall remain unmentioned in this context.

Archaeology has become very specialized in its attention to different time frames in cultural history: it covers prehistory and early history as well as classical archaeology, the Middle Ages and the Modern Era and industrial archaeology. Hence office archaeology can be seen as a sub-discipline of industrial archaeology that focuses on social science questions.

The Anthropology Aspect
Anthropology studies man's tribal history and ancestry as well as our development and ontogeny. Even if certain transportation options appear effective for the masses and worth striving for in our automobile age, or even seem to exclude all other possibilities (even to buy the unavoidable pack of cigarettes at a kiosk) they have not yet led us to give up our innate biped habits. Now, even the "office homo sapiens" seems to be falling back into habits that were considered a thing of the past – due to the seemingly definitive course of cultural evolution and social development. It is obvious that a boy is hidden in every man and that a territorial being lies hidden in every man. This fencing off of territory is expressed in every aspect of life: how else can the survival of a hunting fence in the middle of suburban terraced housing be explained, or the tendency to prefer the parking space close to our home, under the street light for the family car – within the field of vision of the living room window, if

possible. Social interaction is, not least of all, and exciting interplay of nearness and narrowness. Identity as being one's self is the basis for identification (along with an occupation, a group, a conviction, etc.) and requires fencing off from strangers.

The Anthropological and Archaeological Workplace Analysis

Normally the cultural historical analytical view only notices a phenomenon when it is threatened with extinction. In a priori terms, this doesn't seem to be case nor does it seem desirable for work as a field of research – although this case is more of a confirmation of the rule than the exception, since the world of work is undergoing rapid change. Almost all known and common patterns are being questioned and statements – such as the goal of full employment – are increasingly articulated in a conjunctive tense in political rhetoric. Although the creation of life employment accounts suggests different time budgets in which gainful employment times are quantifiable, one glance at real living shows that the borders between working hours and leisure hours are becoming increasingly blurred. In spite of the fact that even consumer habit researchers do not assume that longer opening hours will automatically lead to an increase in turnover, there is hope that greater flexibility will lead to an increased "shopping experience." The logical consequence of this removal of barriers not only affects the patterns of interaction of the acting and reacting persons, it is also manifested in the world of objects. The spectrum ranges from specially designed home office furniture that can be integrated in a private living space to the "living room conversion" of office furnishings. The specific culture of things in the office world reaches beyond the primary objective – making work possible – to a secondary functional level that emphatically addresses the desire for representation and identification. Similar aspects can also be registered in the field of more refined office architecture as a logical consequence. However, the described mechanisms of distinction aren't contemporary phenomena. After all, clerks in the 19th century had the possibility of ascribing rank by either sitting or not sitting, or with backrests of differing heights. These were manifestations made with objects that amounted to a code universally understood.

It is undoubtedly impossible to lump – or clump – all office employees together. On one hand, office work is seen as a mass culture phenomena, on the other hand, an analytical view of the office homo sapiens shows that he can choose his field of work more or less freely and also have a major influence on his (architectural) surroundings. While the first group is directed to accept the given conditions, the latter group can invent their working surroundings themselves. But the ingenuity of those who have to accept the given conditions shouldn't be underestimated. They also discover means and ways of removing the sense of foreignness from their workspace. A casual examination of everyday work shows that the variety of systems of order is at least as large as the fantasy of order avoidance: in the form of the office employee, the primeval hunter and collector seems to continue with his

mischief, completely unconcerned with the evolution of technology and the innumerable time and self-management seminars that are available. Even now with office communication networks, which were initially praised for being paper-free, you find more or less neatly stacked mountains of files on surfaces that were originally defined as work surfaces by ergonomics experts and architects. Precisely measured work surfaces at the ideal height become a playground for cuddly toys and a biotope for coffee mugs. The description of the behavioral patterns surrounding the consumption of hot beverages alone would fill pages and offer highly interesting insights on the meaning of informal and non-verbal workspace communication. Nothing is more cleansing, except for the pleasance of cleaning your ears with Q-tips than the heartfelt tossing of a stack of files into a wastebasket. The walls and moats of files that develop from unrelated processes during individual bureaucratic battles – located on window sills and die tables – only seem threatened by window cleaners who periodically maraud through the building with the merciless intention of cleaning in officially scheduled intervals. This tendency to create barriers is manifested in a thoroughly useful form of territorial behavior in the earliest phases of evolution, which was of elementary importance in defining the border between one's own and someone else's. Thus the foreignness of stone gray of office surroundings is countered with different patterns of action that make the personal appropriation of the workplace possible. Catalysts are created this way that trigger identification with the workplace and with the job itself that also generate long-term revenue. Hence the office becomes at the same a surface for representation and a communication platform for everyday social interaction along with its primary function as a workplace.

The newest research completed in America shows that the home office user satisfaction is definitely not higher than that of normal office employees. On the contrary, the clear separation – also physical spatial separation – of work, leisure and sleeping segments is an advantage for family surroundings. Cheers to those who belong to the species of "inventors," who can go to work and invent their own workplace even at an architectural level. The users of "the unit work surfaces" do indeed seem to have a great will to design and great design competence. This is the case with both the reflection of company philosophy basics (e.g. transparency, clarity, precision in a law firm) and the work methodology requirements (e.g. increasing each others level of information at a company's headquarters) within the architecturally designed space. The unconventional approach that was taken in finding forms naturally lead to polarization among the users: as time passes and the forces of personnel fluctuation take effect, an open space office with a roughly 20 meter-long desk with space for almost as many workplaces will be occupied by a clientele of employees that will not only accept this work situation, but will also identify its particularly pleasing and useful aspects. Naturally the single workspace is subject to increased visual monitoring in this situation, since the bordering space between neighbors is especially low. However, if this is coupled with business

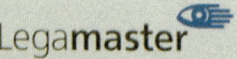

JANUAR 2003 FEBRUAR 2003 MÄRZ 2003 APRIL 2003 MAI 2003 JUNI 2003

JULI 2003 AUGUST 2003 SEPTEMBER 2003 OKTOBER 2003 NOVEMBER 2003 DEZEMBER 2003

management that is sensitized in terms of corporate sociological conditions – as is the case here – the "mass" seated on the ultra-long (community) desk signalizes social awareness and readiness to speak, making the table both a desk and a workbench for the soul. After all, the state of a desk also allows for conclusions about the prevailing work situation: A desk loaded with files shouldn't only be interpreted as a notorious collector's workspace, it could also be a signal for the employee's permanent sense of being overburdened, which could probably be alleviated by changing work processes or responsibilities.

Synopsis

However, by rule, office work remains a mass phenomenon that is met with mass prefabrication today. The respective approaches to solutions depend on the corresponding level of research and fashion currents. At the moment, the combined offices developed in Scandinavia in which a jointly used central area complements the close quarters of individual workplaces are fashionable. These spaces contain technical work tools that can also be used by other employees (e.g. photo copier, fax machine) as well as facilities such as a kitchenette for coffee making, which lead to a (desired) increase in informal communication between colleagues who occupy individual offices when used as a community. Additionally, aspects that have nothing to do with the actual task should be taken into consideration when designing office architecture. The degree to which fire hazard protection or escape route guidelines influence the spatial freedom of architectural design should not be underestimated and they have a considerable influence on the materials that can be used. Another remarkable aspect is the field of acoustics, after all the goal is to make communication possible, but also to reduce the range of sound waves to the point in which working next to each other is possible as well as working with each other. This has even more validity in a time in which constant accessibility has become a sign of quality and status and in which polyphony has received an entirely new meaning: namely simultaneous accessibility via fixed network and mobile phones. This leads to completely absurd communication systems. It turns a car into a personal mobile office, or an ICE train compartment featuring a PC connection into an open space office, it also makes every sidewalk café a forum that is suitable for the discussion of internal company matters. The surrounding crowds of people thus become acoustic insulation and also become accomplices because they are forced to hear what is being said. The field of acoustic spatial design that makes targeted communication possible while reducing background noise is increasingly important in a time defined by the collection and circulation of information and in which verbal communication is relied on more frequently.

After all, the expansion of work into the virtual space is a current time signal. This first af all referse to the organization of the immediate workspace. The work surface the PC rests on becomes a communication platform and work archive at the same time. Then comes the networking of workplaces among each other, which gives an insight into the field of communications architecture whose importance can be underestimated in architecture for work today by offering communication via email and Internet access. The population's reading competence is being subject to an elementary change. Although there is no threat of extinction for readers at the moment, the habits of handling and using texts – and consequently information architecture – are changing. Today's globalizing world especially needs to develop systems of symbols that are unmistakable, since communication isn't what "goes out," it is what "arrives." The highly specialized tele-coaching market has developed in the consulting field that offers additional advisory consulting competence via phone conversations or an Internet chat just in time, so to speak. The possible ramifications of this development for architectural design, can only be speculated on at this point.

In any case, the facts and interesting elements in the field of office archaeology, which was only sketched out roughly here, show that it is a truly broad field. This isn't surprising since work has taken up a considerable amount of our time since we were chased out of paradise. What remains is the hope that in the era of CAD technology, architecture will not be merely understood as the reading of scores of floor plans in accordance with DIN-standards. Instead, it should be a UNIT: it should be the creativity of multidimensional spatial design taking the factors of light, color, sound, smell and surface into consideration – created by people and most of all, for (working) people. A wonderful discussion could be started on whether being is defined by its knowledge or if knowledge defines being. What can be feared is that the necessity for truly human workplace environment design will be recognized less frequently in a time when having a workplace is considered a luxury by most. After all, the army of qualified persons who would like to become employees is a widely available and consequently willing resource.

*Matthias Henkel
Berlin, 2003

*Matthias Henkel studied ethnology, prehistory, early history, botany, and worked in a variety of landmark preservation fields, at the university and furthering education. He is currently the head of the public relations for the State Museums of Berlin.

working

when	1998
where	vienna – austria
client	freimüller / noll / obereder / pilz lawyers
quantity	1
altitude above sea level	176.30 m
coordinates	48° 15' n 16° 25' e
weight	389.40 tons
total payload	71.50 tons
capacity	25 persons
construction time	372h15min
security options	middle

when	1996
where	vienna – austria
client	creditanstalt investmentbank
quantity	1
altitude above sea level	171.80 m
coordinates	48° 15' n 16° 25' e
weight	3321.50 tons
total payload	1625.20 tons
capacity	250 persons
construction time	2041h22min
security options	high

ca investmentbank

ca investmentbank

when	2002 – 2003
where	all over austria
client	generali versicherung ag
quantity	4
altitude above sea level	117.30 – 714.20 m
coordinates	47° 20' n 13° 20' e
weight	512.30 tons
total payload	62.60 tons
capacity	40 persons
construction time	344h25min
security options	middle
graphic design	section.d

generali

04 kundenbetreuer
grundtner hannes
koller juergen

08

when	2001
where	vienna – austria
client	wienerberger ag
quantity	1
altitude above sea level	311.20 m
coordinates	48° 15' n 16° 25' e
weight	1348.50 tons
total payload	607.10 tons
capacity	210 persons
construction time	1987h43min
security options	high

when	2002
where	vösendorf / scs – austria
client	interio
quantity	1
altitude above sea level	194.30 m
coordinates	48° 07' n 16° 20' e
weight	176.80 tons
total payload	103.75 tons
capacity	55 persons
construction time	346h 57min
security options	high
graphic design	section.d

when	2000
where	vienna – austria
client	lansky & prohaska lawyers
quantity	2
altitude above sea level	171.40 m
coordinates	48° 15' n 16° 25' e
weight	1322.70 tons
total payload	326.30 tons
capacity	55 persons
construction time	1495h50min
security options	middle

when	2000
where	vienna – austria
client	association of the austrian wood industries
quantity	1
altitude above sea level	172.10 m
coordinates	48° 15' n 16° 25' e
weight	642.70 tons
total payload	78.20 tons
capacity	30 persons
construction time	356h09min
security options	middle

wood industries

when	1991
where	spittal / drau – austria
client	ilbau gesmbh
quantity	1
altitude above sea level	561.45 m
coordinates	46° 47' n 13° 29' e
weight	14024.90 tons
total payload	3772.20 tons
capacity	650 persons
construction time	12481h20min
security options	high
ceramic door handle	margit denz

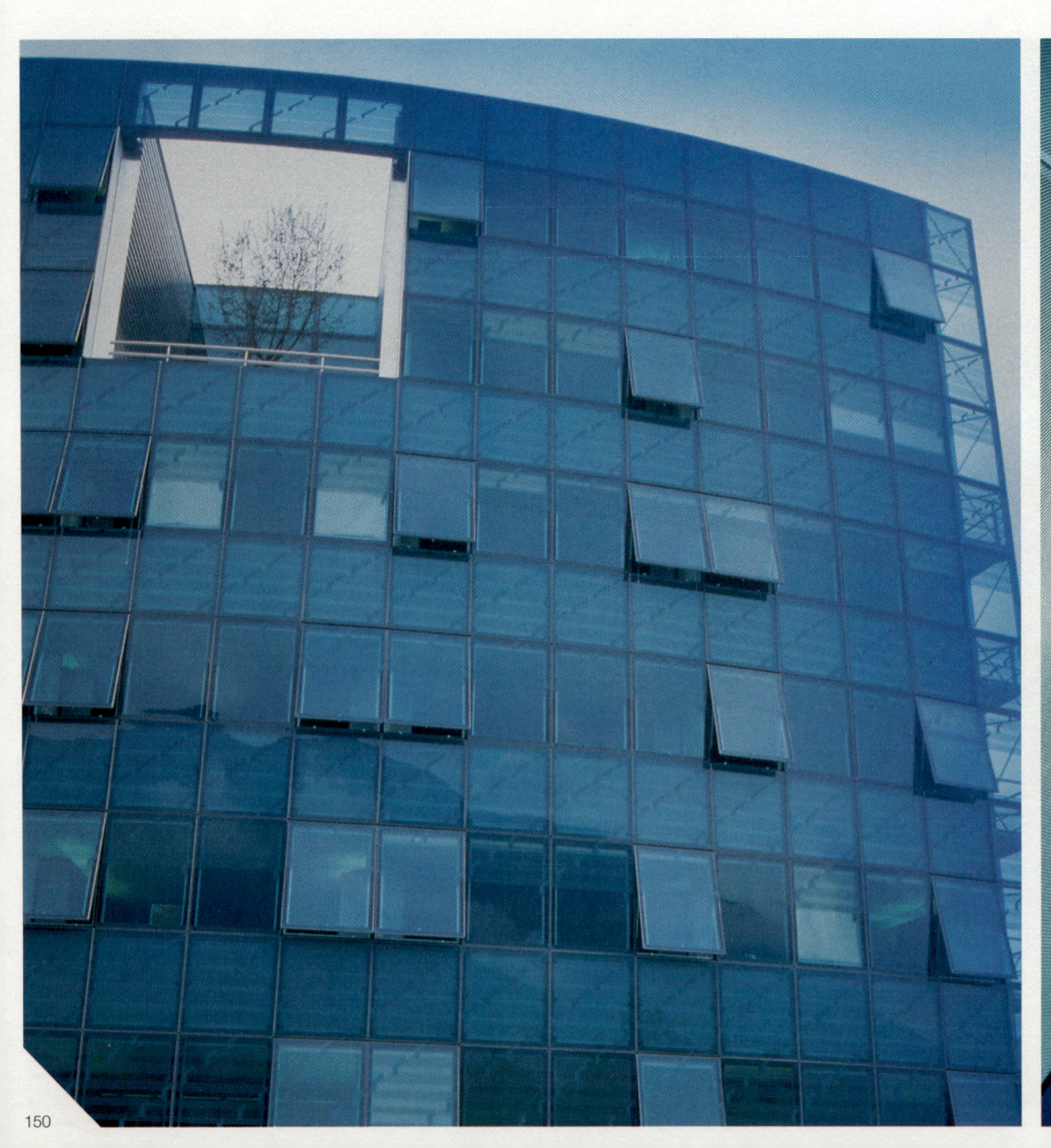

dead loads. the weight of materials of construction incorporated into the building, including but not limited to walls, floors, roofs, ceilings, stairways, built-in partitions, finishes, cladding and other similarly incorporated architectural and structural items, and fixed service equipment, including the weight of cranes.

a method of proportioning structural members and their connections using load and resistance factors such that no applicable limit state is reached when the structure is subjected to appropriate load combinations.

any wall that is not a load-bearing wall. section 1603 construction documents 1603.1 general.

loads and forces for occupancies or uses not covered in this chapter shall be subject to the approval of the building official.

1604.3 serviceability.

rigid elements that are assumed not to be a part of the lateral-force-resisting system shall be permitted to be incorporated into buildings provided that their e... on the action of the system is considered and provided for in design.

1605.3 load combinations using allowable stress design. 1605.3.1 basic load combinations.

100percentwarehousing

Pragmatic Buildings

Is absolutely any building a piece of architecture? The obvious answer would seem to be no. A desert island shelter hastily erected by the fortunate survivor of a shipwreck is going to be a purely practical structure. It has a simple job to do and there is no need—or opportunity—for its form or finish to express any fancy ideas. The materials used will have been whatever was available, chosen for accessibility and practicality, not for aesthetic impact. However, to extend the analogy of the shelter a little further, if two such structures were built by two people (each unaware of the other's presence) at different ends of the same shipwreck island, these buildings would probably differ in small but revealing ways. After a few weeks, with no rescue ship on the horizon, each solitary survivor might start to personalise his or her shelter, adding small features, some reference to home or some token of faith or hope. Distinctions would start to emerge and those distinctions might be seen as the first stirrings of an architectural sense. But does that make it architecture'?

A debate that emerged at the end of the 20th century asked the same basic question about industrial buildings in general and warehouse sheds in particular. They were just boxes. Developers began to wonder whether architects had anything to contribute to the new generation of distribution "supersheds" where the emphasis was almost exclusively on cost efficiency. Did the public need to be addressed in any way by these purely functional buildings? Probably not. Consumers, after all, only visited the retail type of shed where style, marketing and advertising certainly were necessary. But the prefabricated warehouse/distribution shed was a different matter. By the late 1990s this building form was often the product of standardised computer-aided design, a process that relegated planners and architects to supporting roles.

"Well, you are just building boxes," admitted Christopher Merrill of Heitman Financial, part of the Central European Industrial Development Company – CEIDCO – formed with TKG International. Meanwhile John Kontrabecki, president of TKG, allowed that distribution facilities had no "sex appeal", making it difficult to get architects interested.

Ironically things had been very different a quarter of a century before. The classic exercise in giving sheds and boxes sex appeal had come with the famous series of American buildings by the practice S.I.T.E. (Sculpture In The Environment) for its client Best Products Co. Inc. This catalogue showroom merchandiser had no real need to make its boxlike showrooms anything other than plain warehouses for goods which sold themselves rather in the manner of present-day outlets. However, the patronage of the art-loving Best store owners gave S.I.T.E. rare license to create a series of spectacularly eye-catching buildings characterised by cascading bricks, impossible tilted planes, punctured walls and, in one case, a brick façade that appeared to be peeling away from the main structure. Designed to be noticed from a speeding automobile, these were buildings that by virtue of their purpose had been banished to anonymous tracts of real estate where planning permission for eye-catching adventures in style was easily granted. Technically retail stores, they were really warehouses to which the public was initially attracted simply by price. Their fame became global as S.I.T.E.'s Best stores became pin-ups in the world's magazines and newspaper supplements. In fact nothing about the treatment of the buildings expressed anything about the stock inside: the exercise was simply an opportunity for S.I.T.E. principals James Wines and Alison Sky to use hitherto bland, boxy buildings as, well, as sculpture in the environment. By 1977 their Best series reached a pinnacle with the so-called "Notch" showroom in Sacramento, California. Having moved beyond playing tricks with existing boxes, the practice was now building them from scratch and was therefore able to take the trompe l'oeil tricks a stage further. Apparently constructed out of brick, this particular box had a fragmented wedge-shaped lower corner that could break away, moving to open and

close the store. The 45-ton brick-faced wedge was mechanised and mounted on rails and frequently drew applause from the crowds who arrived to see the structure "open" in a morning. This and other Best showrooms flourished throughout 1970s in the backwaters of Virginia, Texas, Iowa, Maryland, Connecticut and California. Since then S.I.T.E. has done few such projects in the US. "Developer mentality here is inclined towards cost" reports James Wines. "In Japan, France and Canada however, they realised that there were profits to be gained by developing a recognisable image".

A decade after S.I.T.E.'s high-profile achievement in the USA, Foster Associates completed the award-winning Renault Distribution Centre, located in a business park on the outskirts of the unglamorous town of Swindon, England. The building represented a bold new change of direction for Foster who, along with Richard Rogers (when they were working together as part of Team 4), had already built a factory for Reliance Controls as well as the Fred Olsen Passenger Terminal building at Milwall Docks, London. The Fred Olsen building deserves a brief special mention, occupying as it does a unique role in the annals of industrial buildings. At the time the Fred Olsen Shipping Line's main trade was carrying a mixed cargo to the Canary Islands and returning with a cargo of bananas. To get maximum use from their ships, Olsen combined this trade with cruises, integrating these two apparently conflicting functions in a complementary way. The Passenger Terminal simply had to extend the ships' practice of keeping the two activities separate. To achieve this Foster deployed a set of 'tubes' to protect passengers from the industrial activities of the quayside and delivering them to their ship without interfering with loading or unloading on the dock. Like the ships themselves, the terminal separated passengers above from freight below.

The Renault Distribution Centre, while inheriting many of the lessons of integration and separation from the Reliance and Fred Olsen projects, ultimately added a sense of playfulness that would never recur in Foster's impressive catalogue of work. It rejected the traditional idea of hiding the warehouse behind a glamorous office frontage and then tucking in other services and departments wherever they might fit. Foster, already a social engineer in architect's clothing, put warehouse, offices, training school, workshops and a restaurant under the democratic embrace of a single roof, combining them even as he separated them. Comprising four parallel rows of 24m modules, the Renault Centre also featured coloured car body shells suspended from the ceiling and rooflights positioned to give views of the complex roofscape from inside the building. Its suspended roof sections were supported by cable-stayed steel masts painted "Renault" yellow that successfully evoked the client's corporate image without the need for traditional signage.

By the end of the 20th century, some of Foster's preoccupations with Renault were still looking valid. Merrill and Kontrabecki of CEIDCO were starting to acknowledge that certain architects were, after all, crucial to the construction of even the most cost-conscious distribution centre. Their Warsaw Distribution Centre by Stefan Kurylowicz Architects prompted Kontrabecki to say "I try to use local suppliers, materials and subcontractors necessary to create a real estate product that is economical to build and of good quality. To do that you need to have the guidance of an architect who understands both worlds. Stefan Kurylowicz is one of the few who does."

Kurylowicz himself noted that there was a trend towards combining warehouse and HQ "whether as two separate entities or the same building."

Distribution needs were also changing as retail patterns shifted in response to new technology and consumer tastes. Warehouses were now often more than simple storage buildings because since the mid 1980s, changes in the distribution chain

Pragmatic Buildings

had demanded corresponding logistical changes in many sectors. The emergent "Just-In-Time" philosophy has resulted in smaller in-store inventories, smaller order sizes, closer ties between manufacturer and retailer and a need for faster delivery systems. All this made demands on buildings that once had been little more than giant storage sheds but could now be an active, organic part of the distribution and retail process. This shift has brought its own advantages and problems. In the UK and many parts of Europe, nothing could be further from today's industrial storage needs than the received image of the huge Victorian warehouses. Not a year passes that some giant 19th century structure originally designed to generate power or store sugar is adapted to become a very different sort of space; the warehouse as monument is no longer a relevant model in a very different commercial world. More recently Norman Foster, now knighted and elevated in international reputation, recommitted his practice to "intelligent" industrial buildings when it designed the HACTL Superterminal 1 at Chek Lap Kok Hong Kong International Airport—a huge distribution shed, designed to function in 24-hour working shifts, all year round with the capacity to handle 2.5 million tonnes of cargo per annum and a two-kilometre air-side terminal interface for maximum ease of access to cargo. This is an example of a cargo terminal as mini city, with logistical challenges to match and the organisational power of a central computing system developed and marketed by the client. As a balancing act between demanding logistics and elegant formal solutions, HACTL Superterminal 1 demonstrates that a shed – albeit a vast and complex one – can indeed claim to be industrial architecture of the highest order. Nor is it unique. Many predictions for the future envisage a move away from road haulage and towards airfreight, bringing with it a demand for similar facilities that could be as large as 2 million square feet and sited at or near to air terminals. Even so, such is the vitality of international commerce, that distribution centres are still springing up along major transport routes the world over, reasserting them as part of the landscape for car and train travellers. As such they are potentially ideal billboards, three-dimensional marketing tools and giant display objects. Looked at this way, the design of a building itself may not need to be elaborate or dramatic, simply practical—as long as the external display opportunities are grasped. Large-scale text and images, logos and illustrations can all be introduced.

In fact the challenge of architecturally integrating images and text into the surface of buildings is one that can now be met with ever more sophisticated technology. The simple wrapping solution, still used with success when temporarily shrouding buildings under construction, is essentially a solution from the display industry. Now it is increasingly possible to integrate quality images into glass and other façades and this falls quite naturally within the remit of the architect, should he or she choose to embrace it. An exposed etched image may create maintenance problems but it is also possible to sandwich decorative laminate between sheets of glass, providing a cleanable surface and endless communication possibilities.

Prague's Zlaty Andel Building in by Jean Nouvel used self-adhesive foil-cut vinyl to apply a huge image and graphics to the facade. Architect MSSI also used vinyl for Cinven's (a financial services company) Main Tower in Frankfurt, decorating a glass wall on both faces of the building with graphic quotations in a variety of typefaces. Tim Webb-Jenkins, graphic designer on the project, maintained that: "Graphics have a big contribution to make to the built environment, (something) which is often missed by architects whose preoccupation is with other issues".

If a financial services building is not exactly a warehouse, it does at least house an intangible service. In this respect it resembles distribution centres where specialised components may be stored, shipped or tested, but where the public would still have some difficulty recognising a finished product. At Støvring, Demark, factory for the membrane switch division of Danish electronics firm Mekoprint cleverly reflected the

pliable sheets of circuitry that sit invisibly inside all manner of electronic gadgets such as mobile phones and microwave ovens. Architect Henning Larsen came up with a way of using the distinctive membrane switch pattern hugely enlarged and screen-printed onto the glazed façade of the building.

The effect, when viewed from the outside, is a strongly-defined glass wall that illustrates the seductively abstract product while workers inside benefit from random shading provided by the giant screen print. The overall result is an exemplary instance of a building where graphic design, advertising and architecture have been fused together. Without the screen-printed imagery, not only would the building project a very different image externally, the actual experience of working in it would be different. The traditional practice of applying or appending large-scale graphics to buildings gives way to integrating them into the structural fabric. It is ironic that it should be the industrial building – the poor relation of "grand" architecture and frequently regarded as hardly being architecture at all – that has encouraged this process. What is more, the potential of treating buildings in this way goes beyond the occasional adventure in enlivening a drab industrial landscape with a jazzy façade. When previously separate disciplines come together, there is usually some degree of cross-fertilisation that will change them all to a greater or lesser degree. The classic example of this phenomenon in recent years has nothing to do with the built environment and everything to do with an age of rapid, technologically-driven change. In the last two decades of the 20th century the digital revolution saw the coming together of broadcast & movies, print & publishing and the computer industry. Each had its own traditions and technology, its own well-worn routes to success and even its own vocabulary. Each would have continued down its own path, resisting change and clinging to the practices of the past had it not been for the irresistible impact of the digital revolution which imposed the new methods and manners of a shared technological culture on all of them.

Everything changed: in publishing many support industries disappeared overnight; in movies, computer-generated images gave birth to new genres just as they rendered the old optical special effects obsolete; digital broadcasting introduced consumer interactivity along with significant technical improvements. A new generation of people began to work in those industries, freed from restrictive practices and in tune with new technologies.

It is not entirely fanciful to see similar possibilities for change in architecture, even if advertising and graphic design are by their nature, less likely to change as the result of any coming together.

The industrial building – warehouse, distribution centre, logistics shed or storage space – represents something of a blank canvas for the imaginative architect. Freed by context from the constraints of protected city centres or restricted residential zones, the industrial building can be in the avant-garde if the developer/client is willing. Two decades ago, the British architectural press was filled with images of new distribution centres located in places that to most people existed only as names on road signs. While entrenched architectural camps argued endlessly about extensions to London's National Gallery in Trafalgar Square, exciting new buildings were sprouting on the outskirts of undistinguished British provincial towns that had been chosen as sites for distribution centres simply because of their proximity to major transport routes.

Interesting as many of these buildings were, most were constrained by "pure" architectural thinking. Young architects were designing them in a feisty spirit of modernism that contrasted deliberately with the parallel trend for building out-of-town supermarkets in a folksy vernacular style, all mock gables and traditional

warehousing

pitched roofs expanded to accommodate thousands of square metres of food retailing. Even the best of those new industrial buildings seemed to be part of an ongoing closed-circuit architectural debate that reflected the ideological conflict between traditionalists and modernists. It was a debate that found echoes in the older cities of the United States (where a paucity of old buildings often intensified the wish to create "traditional" style buildings) although, encouragingly, this debate seemed to exercise many European countries rather less. In any case, there were few industrial buildings anywhere that incorporated commercial messages to the public; there was no one thinking like S.I.T.E. had done a decade before, and even they had been content to grab the public's attention without tailoring a client-specific message. Even Norman Foster, who had hung coloured automobile shells from the roof of the Renault Centre in the 80s, lamented that the elegant interior of his 1991 Stansted Airport building would probably soon be ruined by unconsidered advertisements and garish café parasols. Although there was no architectural control over what paying tenants might do to their rented concourse space, it is interesting to consider how Stansted might have differed if it had been conceived in a cultural climate where "subsidiary" commercial interests were addressed as part of the overall design.

How then might such a climate emerge, now that we have embarked on the 21st century in a spirit of buoyant globalisation where logos and brands predominate and shopping has been elevated almost to a philosophy? To put it another way, what is wrong with architecture that fast-track communications thinking might put right?

Well, architecture is traditionally seen as an expensive, monumental and "permanent" public activity, while graphic design and advertising are responsive, fast, fashionable and ephemeral. Could architecture be like them? If so, would this be desirable? In his classic serio-comic 1950 book "Parkinson's Law", C. Northcote Parkinson presented a sustained conceit arguing that whenever a company finally acquired the perfectly-designed building in which to conduct its business, that company was almost certainly on the point of collapse. He cited numerous examples, all of which claimed to illustrate that any company or organization's best work was done in uncomfortable, unsuitable, makeshift buildings and that the purpose-built, triumphal architecture always came far too late.

The influential British architect Cedric Price, born in 1934, has long argued against the aesthetics-driven dogma of expensive, monumental and permanent architecture. He has always championed the idea that buildings should be made of lightweight, flexible, demountable components that encourage a responsive approach to the built environment. In this approach change and demolition take the place of preservation and permanence. A typical Cedric Price scheme might propose a series of short-life structures intended to operate as urban levers, valves, platforms and conduits that would generate new types of views, retreats, aspects and information access. Price's commitment to the organic process of urban design rather than the restrictive formal nature of its buildings contrasted markedly with the efforts of a generation of architects who saw their early idealism eroded by working with the status quo rather than outside of it. Despite a number of built projects, Price has generally worked outside of the status quo, always embracing new technology and always mistrusting the cult of the Architect with the Great Reputation.

Now the new generation of warehouses and their contemporary companion structures – distribution centres, cargo terminals, logistics centres, computer server sheds, high-tech manufacturing and storage plants – seem to offer new possibilities that are perhaps unexpectedly in tune with Price's approach. As we have seen, once the industrial storage building was a monument to commercial achievement, a symbol of permanence built at a time when industrial dynasties grew and prospered

at a glacial speed. Now, in an age when businesses amalgamate, reform and disappear with sometimes alarming rapidity, there is more than a trace of Ozymandian hubris about those cavernous Victorian warehouses and market halls whose fabric endured way beyond their need and which are now redeployed as shopping malls, art galleries and "heritage experience" attractions. Today's storage and distribution solutions should have no aspirations to being like their forbears any more than the latest Nike TV commercial should have any expectation of being cherished through the centuries as classic moviemaking. Instead the new industrial buildings simply need to be a vital link in some contemporary manufacturing chain, well suited to their purpose, economical to build and alive to their unique opportunity to communicate something distinctive to the public.

Twenty years ago the best an industrial building could hope for was to send out the signal that the client or tenant was a champion of high-tech or otherwise radical architecture. That message might impress or alienate, depending on a whole raft of public feelings (or lack of them) about architecture, the environment, historicism and nostalgia, but it rarely said anything about the nature of the business being conducted within. However, today it seems more natural to build industrial buildings efficiently and to use a new breed of architects who do not indulge in self-aggrandising gestures but who instead relish the task of responding to the Zeitgeist with tools familiar from other disciplines: logos, text, colour and evocative imagery. The functionality of such buildings is of course taken for granted, but in many cases it simply does not require any architect to reinvent this particular wheel. Instead it requires him to integrate personal touches that tell the public something about the organization and its activities. Technology now provides techniques to make those touches part of the holistic whole, not glued-on slogans or temporary window displays. The public is now visually far more literate than ever before and more sceptical too, so the frames of visual reference should shift from yesterday's pretentious and mock-classical (where crass things like bas relief representations of Atlas shouldering the world are meant to signify global power) towards more flexible and accessible contemporary imagery. There is of course also room for genuinely innovative warehouse, distribution centre and cargo handling building designs when new internal systems and external envelopes really are required. No one would wish the architect to become a mere decorator of prefabricated buildings and systems; however, many might fervently wish the architect to approach such buildings as a communications professional, someone with as much appetite and skill for tapping into the public mood as the best advertising creative or a graphic designer. The result may not only be better industrial buildings more suited to their purpose, but also a new and more dynamic strand of creative thinking running through all of contemporary architecture, an architecture less rooted in the traditions of the past and more in tune with the impulses of contemporary society.

*Graham Vickers
Watford, 2003

*Graham Vickers is a freelance writer on design, architecture and advertising.
He has contributed to many international magazines and his books include "Style In Product Design" and "Key Moments in Architecture".
In 2002 he co-authored the book "Rewind: 40 Years of Design and Advertising" for Phaidon.

when	1992
where	berlin – germany
client	ilbau gesmbh
quantity	1
altitude above sea level	70.35 m
coordinates	52° 31' n 13° 22' e
weight	7823.50 tons
total payload	3165.20 tons
capacity	180 persons
construction time	10422h15min
security options	high

ilbau technology park berlin

ilbau technology park berlin

when	1994
where	ansfelden – austria
client	rewe – billa ag
quantity	1
altitude above sea level	290.60 m
coordinates	48° 12' n 14° 17' e
weight	10556.40 tons
total payload	7869.70 tons
capacity	600 persons
construction time	3921h45min
security options	high
colour concept	irena rosc

central billa fresh specialties warehouse

central billa fresh specialties warehouse

when	2002
where	vienna – austria
client	telekom austria ag
quantity	1
altitude above sea level	223.10 m
coordinates	48° 15' n 16° 25' e
weight	11697.50 tons
total payload	3765.00 tons
capacity	500 persons
construction time	3005h30min
security options	high
colour concept	irena rosc

telekom logistics center

telekom logistics center

when	1999
where	linz – austria
client	voest alpine ag
quantity	1
altitude above sea level	260.55 m
coordinates	48° 18' n 14° 17' e
weight	55143.50 tons
construction time	1007h14min
security options	high

voest alpine steel

voest alpine steel

gross leasable area. the total floor area designed for tenant occupancy and exclusive use.

402.5.1 minimum width. the minimum width of the mall shall be 20 fee (6000 mm).

the covered mall building shall be equipped throughout with a standpipe system as required by section 905.3

402.9 smoke control.

foam plastics used in signs shall have flame- retardant characteristics such that the sign has a maximum heat- release rate of 150 kilowatts when tested in accordance with ul 1975 and the foam plastics shall h the physical characteristics specified in this section.

3. ventilation and automatic fire detection equipment for smokeproof enclosures.

3. the adjacent spaces of any three floors of the atrium shall not be required to be separated from the atrium where such spaces are included in computing the atrium volume for the design of the smoke control system.

100percentexhibiting

Showcase Magic
The Showcase's Progress from the Museum to the Theme Store

The sale of goods may be facing the greatest revolution in its history. The traditional "store" has received threatening competition, just as the supermarket has. The possibilities offered by tele-shopping – such as automatic search programs that identify the supplier offering the best price within seconds – raise the question of whether retail will be transformed into a computerized delivery service with an integrated marketing agency. To compensate, this scenario is being confronted with themed shopping. To be able to gauge the possibilities of themed shopping and think it through, the first question that should be addressed is what the shopping experience actually consists of. Therefore, it is necessary to hark back and examine a special case among the sales of goods: the museum shop.

The Museum Showcase as an Altar
A museum is a place where things can be seen that are not used in any way. This not only goes for old vessels, tools and tobacco boxes, but also for paintings. They aren't hanging in a museum to decorate its walls; instead the walls of the museum were put up to present the paintings. The things in the museum are only there to be viewed. Showcases are there to insure things aren't touched. Since the things in the museum are not in use, they have no utility value. Nonetheless, they generally have the highest trading value for exactly that reason. They are good examples to demonstrate the mutual independence of utility and trade values with.

However, the history of things removed from use reaches back much further than the invention of the museum. Burial objects are the oldest objects that bear testament to human culture. They are always everyday things that were banned from being used. At the same time, grave robbery was considered the worst crime. Hence the ban turned everyday things into holy things. A similar practice can also be seen in the sacrificial offerings in antique temples. Practical things also change, receiving a symbolic context; this is also an instance in which a ban on use creates holiness.

But while the burial objects and sacrificial offerings were indicators for religious systems of meaning, the things we find in a museum that have been withdrawn from use are indicators of historical systems of meaning. It is important to note that the meaning of history is completely unknown and foreign to the things. Museum objects were not made to symbolise the time in which they were produced. Instead, it is our museum culture today that turns old things for everyday use into symbols of history with institutionalised bans on their use.

Not only can we see with these examples that trading value can exist independently from utility value, but also that completely different systems of meaning such as religion, sacrificial rituals, the cult of the dead, history, aesthetics, as well as prestige, a passion for collecting, the presentation of the spoils of a victory, accumulating treasures and prodigality can give things a meaning without implying use.

Things such as the pieces of a game, meaningless black or white chips, but they can become important objects within the rules of a game, of a board game, for example. That's the case with all signs. The letter "A" has no meaning of its own, but it has a lot of meaning in the context of the alphabet. The "A" only has a meaning within the system of differences to the other letters in the alphabet. The same combination of lines could note another tone in another alphabet. Then the "A" would be a "B," the same way an altar can be torn out of the context of its meaning

in a church and set up in a museum. Then it isn't an altar anymore, it is a work of art. The altar hasn't changed, but the rule of interpretation changed from a religious system of meaning to an artistic system of meaning.

Museologists always tell the following anecdote: An old peasant woman once kneeled in front of the painting of a saint in a museum only to be told politely by the museum attendant that her behaviour was inappropriate.

What do these removed examples indicate? Things don't have their own characteristics or meanings. Instead, they receive their meaning solely through a code, through cultural interpretation rules. Things have no characteristics, which leads to increasingly different interpretations for the same things in a pluralistic society. The openness of things with regard to competing interpretation systems will become increasingly important for the sale of goods. Another example, when someone goes to McDonalds and eats a hamburger, they can do so to: express the sense of self-loathing they feel at the moment, or to relive the American dream of their schoolboy days. He could also be there to do something forbidden after a week of ascetic health. Or, on the contrary, McDonalds advertising might have convinced him that the combination of meat, bread and salad is the best for his health. Youths go to McDonalds to feel especially mature by going to a restaurant alone; while adults go so they can eat like children again. You can search for superior American hygienic culture at McDonalds, but also escape to a little bit of barbarism from your own sense of civilisation. And you can go there to take pleasure in confirming your own politically/morally-based prejudice that hamburgers simply taste awful. The hamburger itself remains the same, but its interpretations are open to all the randomness of cultural change.

But let's get back to the museum. Imagine the showcase that contains a stone. We are in an exhibition on ancient Egypt. A sign teaches us that this stone sealed the tomb of Tutenkhamen. The sign and the explanation by the museum pedagogue make it an object that deserves to be honoured, but so do the noble museum space, the expensive limelight lamps that make it shine and the photoelectric barrier. These elements keep visitors from approaching the stone too jauntily, as well as the guards, the alarms and the known insurance value: all of these things define the way we experience it, as an object of veneration. If it were placed in a pile of rubble in the courtyard of the museum nobody would ever find it again.

The Museum Shop as a "Culture Store"
We land in the museum shop after taking our walk around the museum shop, where we are confronted with a showcase that also contains said stone, although it can be identified as a copy and has a price tag. But a disgruntled night watchman might have swapped the original for the copy the night before.

Whoever buys a copy in the museum isn't buying it for its utility or trading value. They are buying it to own the symbolic body of meaning developed in the museum. Not the stone, but its meaning is the actual product in terms of the objective of ownership.

But one can also simply interpret a museum shop as a "shop in a museum." However, one can also argue, with certain legitimacy, that a museum with a shop inside isn't a museum in the conventional sense anymore. Instead, it is a new form of shop, a shop with a particularly large shop window and especially complex product presentation interiors. This would mean the consumer society converted the museum into a sales-promoting establishment in the souvenir business. Today's museum is a large, "souvenir shop selling mementos of itself."

Is that an exaggeration? It should be kept in mind that it isn't only museums that are increasingly becoming "shop museums." Museum shops and museum cafes are also beginning to take up more and more museum space, while on the other side, retailers are taking greater pains to present their goods and convey their meaning. So one could speak of a historical convergence, of a mutual approximation and emulation by both institutions: museums and shops.

On Utility and the Usefulness of Things
The idea of utility is the thought that something that functions is something worthy – an understanding typical of our culture. To judge an object by its usefulness is one of the possible interpretations. It requires previous knowledge, a collective background of usefulness. The stone in the museum also demands cultural education on what a museum is and the significance of ancient Egypt to us. Let's take kitchen appliances as a counterexample. Most large food processors and their ten adapters are barely used after they are bought. A toaster indicates a culture that prefers white bread. A wooden knife block that holds ten knives isn't practical. On the contrary, it promises zestful, voluntary kitchen work with its manifold differentiations. It isn't advisable to try to squeeze lemons with Philipp Starck's famous lemon squeezer, which has been on the cover of every kitchen furnishings brochure for years.

The amount of things that are used among those that are purchased isn't very high. But the question of necessity also arises when looking at the things we use daily. All these useful things weren't needed as recently as 200 years ago. That makes it clear that the technology and both its applications and the need for it were invented at the same time. What you need depends on the culture you happen to be in. An ascetic person might think a richly set table is useless, a vegetarian doesn't see any nutritional value in a roast and an arriviste can't see any use in the goods that communicate today's trendy new sense of humility. Terms such as practice, use, utility and function only make sense in predefined fields of action, within existing chains of action.

Just take the simplest kitchen appliance you need on a daily basis, a knife: in Japanese culture, the same knife would have an entirely different meaning and other purposes. Japan has a highly developed cutting culture. Cutting raw materials often replaces cooking; it has the symbolic function of transferring food from nature into culture and is therefore associated with ritualistic considerations. Every cut, of raw fish, for example, represents a small work of art. In our culture, the same knife can be understood as an antiquated precursor to the electric knife. Whether you want to attribute the least bit of usefulness to the electric knife or not, it can be established that the return of the simple, non-electric knife isn't taking place because it is easier to handle, but because the meaning of craftsmanship in cooking is changing currently. Cooking is being upgraded since it isn't associated with the image of a housewife anymore, instead it is linked the image of a chef, of cooking as an artistic hobby, a craft pursued in our spare time.

So the cooking knife and the old stone in the museum have something in common: both have no meaning and no usefulness per se. A bread knife would be as useless as the stone in the museum in a culture in which it is a strict practice to break bread. Things only develop meaning from their context. Things only have uses and meanings within a society's context of action and meaning. Things are merely media that take on conventional meanings. Without agreements on what is considered useful, worth striving for or meaningful, nothing can have a use, value or meaning.

On the Avant-garde of Use and Goods/Things
So it can be said that goods/things are initially merely meaningless playing pieces that acquire meaning within a communication process – the sales process – in this case. The communication itself may seem random from a distance, but it is largely predefined for the individual within the respective cultural framework.

Advertising is understood as a useful means with which to encourage a customer to buy something in a conventional sense. But exactly the opposite follows from what has been said until now: the customer buys goods so he/she can own the image associated with the goods, making it part of him/her. The goods have the same relationship to advertising that a remote control unit has to a television image: they are the part of the viewing experience I can touch with my hand. It is only the material bridge, the medium for the appropriation of impressions and messages. Usefulness and utility are the possible but not necessary messages of things. They aren't significantly different from other contexts of meaning and action in which things and other goods can be put. One buys goods to bring advertising to life. The goods are only the means, or the mediator and conveyor of the impression we have based on the good's advertising.

How does a museum shop manage to sell a stone that could be found on the street at any time for 100 Euros? The museum gives it a context in which it has an indubitable, reliable nature. An art history student guides you through the exhibition who is noticeably infixed in his conviction concerning the importance of Egyptian artistic historical monuments. By the way, occasionally you can find similarly good salespeople in other businesses. A DJ, whom a city's young people know from appearances in various music clubs, works in a record store. He isn't considered a record salesman who occasionally plays records in a discotheque. Instead, he is really considered an authentic person; an example, an opinion leader and expert in a loosely communicating association based on a subculture's values. His credibility comes from overcoming the difference between work and leisure. He only knows one form of action and he defines himself through this lone field of action: he is a DJ – not a person who works as a record salesman. He is similar to Josef Beuys, who wasn't a man who worked as an artist, he was an artist. The same goes for the young art historian that leads us through the museum and explains the great value of our stone. He isn't an employee and citizen who is employed as an exhibition guide. He is an absolute enthusiast and he identifies completely with his duties. Such an authentic salesperson identity is only possible in the narrowest sense of cultural products. Cosmetics salespeople often have faces that are especially appropriate for the job, on which cosmetics are particularly effective. Members of the snowboarding scene work in snowboarding shops, and you can tell they enjoy using the boards themselves on weekends. A car accessory salesman might restore old-timers in his spare time or be a rally driver, or an auto enthusiast.

All of the examples mentioned have in common that they have overcome the old separation between work and leisure roles and that they are the avant-garde in

terms of using the goods they sell. The shop is the stage for this new type of salesman, the "avant-garde user." He is as an especially successful example of self-realization, someone who was able to make his passion his job. The customer buys the goods as a medium through which he can take a piece of the the of the "avant-garde user" home. He buys the record to be a bit of a DJ himself; he buys clothes so he can be as chic as the salesperson. And he buys the extra brake light so he can be part of the world of rally driving and motoring enthusiasts. The buyer wants to identify with what seems to him to be the salesperson's highly authentic way of life by buying the product. The goods are only the mediator that seems to make it possible to symbolically overcome the separation of work and leisure. The modern salesperson is an example of the connection between a person and goods/things, the way a photo model is. The photo model's connection is an exact inverse reflection of the buyer's. While the buyer clings to the goods, the goods cling to the model. By buying the goods, the buyer seeks to acquire a bit of what seems to be the salesperson's successful life, which he envies. The goods are a souvenir that documents a human encounter, a symbol of participation in what he considers the consistent and not at all alien salesperson's existence.

In any case, the goods/things remain mere empty playing pieces that derive meaning and desirability from the respective communication game in which they are used. Although making the goods his property seems to be the goal of his desire, the goods' meaning is the true object of his desire. The goods/thing are only a symbol, the things they symbolise are what is desired. Only within symbolic – and that means communicative – contexts can goods/things become desirable. Desire addresses the goods, but always reaches beyond them. The goods merely symbolise the ideas and the expectations the customer has of them.

Goods as Objects on Display
The goods in a shop window and the museum piece in the showcase have a lot in common. Both are removed from any use at the moment. The goods in the window are already removed from the context of action of their production, without having entered the scope of action related to use. They sit in the window the way a show star stands on the stage. They are removed from everyday life and the bustle of use and are in a purely aesthetic space meant purely for contemplation. In an exhibition, things have the same sacred status; they are pure and innocent, untarnished, perfect and absolute in their selves. The only thing you can do is snatch them away from their "existence for the sake of existing," from their high-handed, useless existence as objects by buying them. The buyer envies the perfection of the goods on display, their completeness and their status as an object of pure admiration. That is why he desires them in their status as an object on display. But as soon as he buys them, he notices that the things become something else by purchasing them. The act of buying them converts them from a glamorous and at the same time museum-like display object, to something that will soon be a worthless, shabby thing that isn't very remarkable anymore in everyday use. A new vacuum cleaner makes you heart race in the shop window, but you prefer to hide it in the closet at home.

The act of buying as a transformation
But it isn't only the goods that change in subjective perception when they are bought. The buyer also changes a little by buying them. Since people define themselves via the goods they are equipped with, the buyer's identity changes with

every purchase – more or less, depending on the significance of the goods. If I buy a Porsche, I become a Porsche driver, and I will have to make an effort to convince my friends that at least I am not a typical Porsche driver. If I buy a chocolate bar, the image I have of myself and that I present to others will change to a smaller degree, at least if I am not a health freak, anorexic or a nature fanatic.

Hence the act of buying something is a double transformation: the thing becomes something else and the buyer becomes someone else. So it is a doubly problematic process that sways both the interior and exterior world a bit. Buying is the de-stabilisation of the ego. You become permeable, open. This is a psychologically delicate operation; it is the interplay of all the most personal emotions that affect the ego and the stabilisation of one's self-image. Thus this process requires a lot of empathy from the salesman for the potential conflicts involved.

If you think back to the old days in which salespeople wore white or blue work clothes and explained how good the value-for-money ratio of every item was with an earnest expression as well as emphasising the high quality, proven and long-lasting materials it was made of and how practical, useful, effort-saving, effective and ingenious it was, you have to say: those salespeople did a good job, even from today's view described earlier. In the culture of the time, buyers thought pretty unanimously that functionality, materiality and effectiveness were important, significant product characteristics worth striving for. The objectivity of the shops then and the salesperson's earnest behaviour were perfect staging elements for this image of goods. There is also a group of buyers who buy goods to cling to the myth of function today. But one shouldn't believe that the belief in need and function is less unreal or illusory than the belief in the indispensability of a major trademark. Goods acquire the meaning they need from their context, from their surroundings, before they appear on the stage of consumption as their representative.

*Wolfgang Pauser
Vienna, 2003

*Wolfgang Pauser was born in Vienna in 1959. He worked as a freelance essayist on the culture of consumption and applied arts for Die Zeit until 1998. He also developed "cultural historical product analysis" and advises companies in corporate culture development matters. His other projects include Dr. Pausers Werbebewusstsein (Dr. Pauser's Consciousness of Advertising, 1995) and thecrystalweb.com, 2003, a virtual museum.

when	2000
where	vienna – austria
client	wienerberger ag
quantity	1
altitude above sea level	315.20 m
coordinates	48° 15' n 16° 25' e
weight	221.30 tons
total payload	62.20 tons
capacity	40 persons
construction time	440h46min
security options	middle

wienerberger showroom

when	2000
where	vienna – austria
client	künstlerhaus, exhibition "den fuss in der tür – manifeste des wohnens"
quantity	1
altitude above sea level	171.50 m
coordinates	48° 15' n 16° 25' e
weight	0.03 tons
construction time	11h15min
security options	low

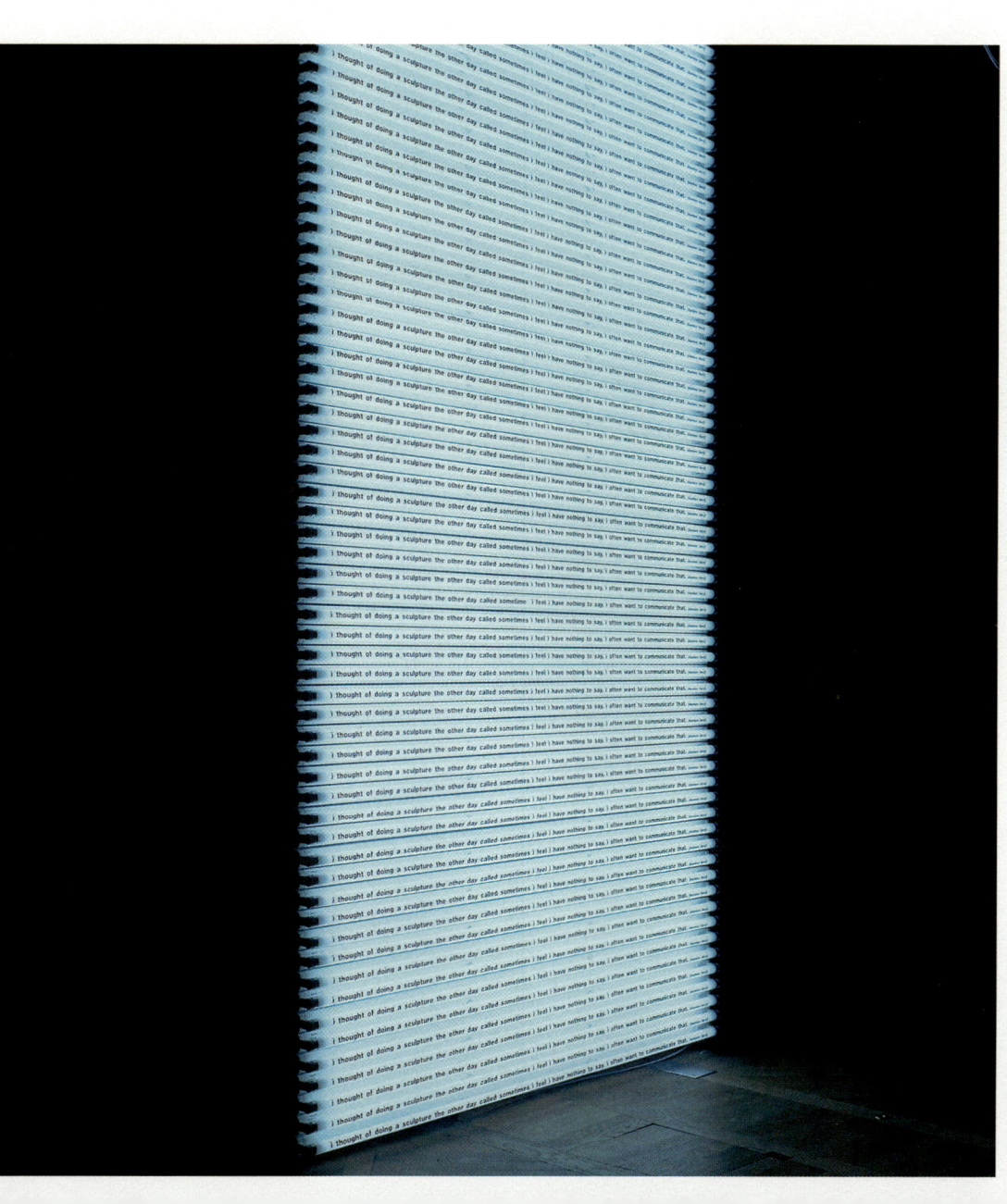

when	2000
where	austria
client	mobilkom austria ag
quantity	1
altitude above sea level	variable
coordinates	48° 15' n 16° 25' e
weight	9.80 tons
total payload	12.00 tons
capacity	40 persons
construction time	122h15min
security options	middle

mobilkom fair stand

when	1998
where	primmersdorf – austria
client	irena rosc
quantity	1
altitude above sea level	380.45 m
coordinates	48° 51' n 15° 34' e
weight	98.30 tons
total payload	73.70 tons
capacity	50 persons
construction time	603h15min
security options	low

silverfish

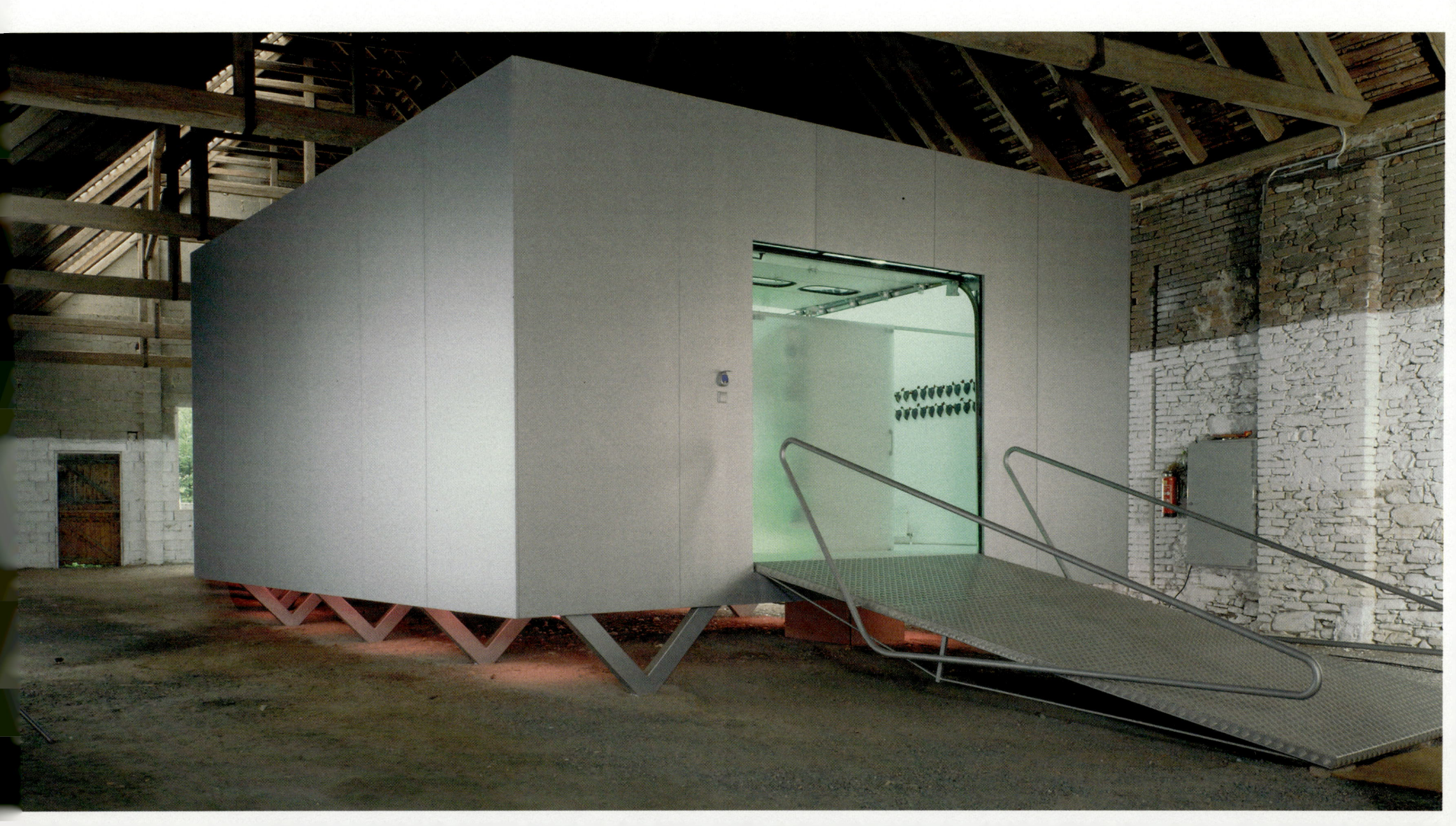

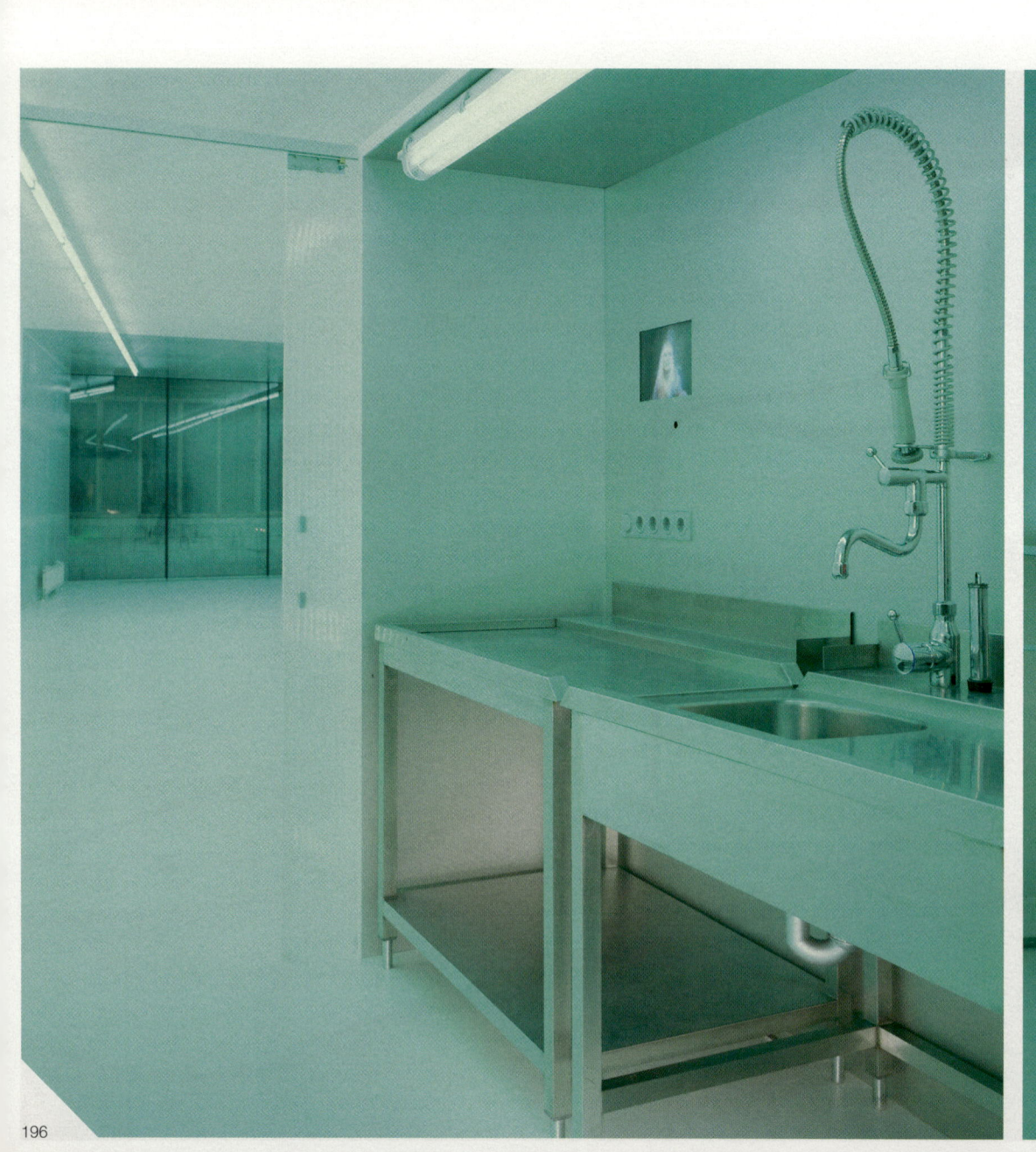

silverfish

when	2000
where	vienna – austria
client	libro ag
quantity	1
altitude above sea level	171.80 m
coordinates	48° 15' n 16° 25' e
weight	9.60 tons
total payload	7.40 tons
capacity	12 persons
construction time	334h12min
security options	low

lion.cc ronacher

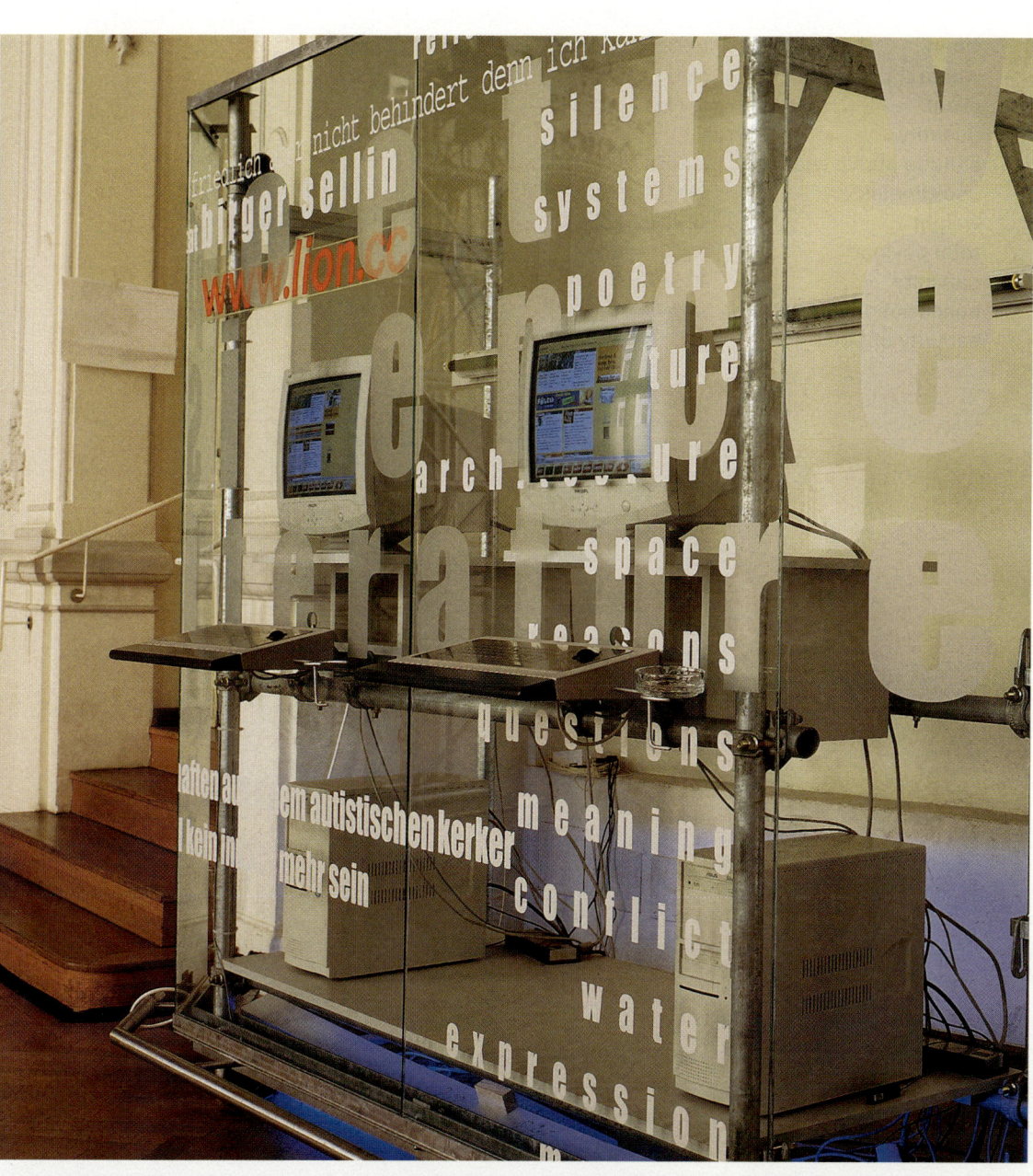

when	1993
where	vienna – austria
client	de haas
quantity	1
altitude above sea level	variable
coordinates	48° 15' n 16° 25' e
weight	12.40 tons
total payload	17.50 tons
capacity	90 persons
construction time	287h49min
security options	low

rainbow collection

rainbow collection

when	1998
where	vienna – austria
client	petrovic
quantity	1
altitude above sea level	161. 90m
coordinates	48° 15' n 16° 25' e
weight	40.80 tons
total payload	4.10 tons
capacity	7 persons
construction time	288h23min
security options	middle

minimal cube

the net free ventilating area shall not be less than1/ 150 of the area of the space ventilated, with 50 percent of the required ventilating area provided by ventilators located in the upper portion of the space to be ventilated at least 3 feet(914 mm) above eave or cornice vents with the balance of the required ventilation provided by eave or cornice vents.

the minimum openable area to the outdoors shall be 4 percent of the floor area being ventilated.

access to mechanical appliances installed inunder- floor areas, in attic spaces and on roofs or elevated structures shall be in accordance with the international mechanical code.

ventilation openings shall be covered for their height and width with any of the following materials, provided that the least dimension of the covering shall not exceed1/ 4 inch(6 mm):

the installation of operable louvers shall not be prohibited.

1. required exterior openings are permitted to open into a roofed porch where the porch: 1.1. abuts a public way, yard or court. 1.2. has a ceiling height of not less than 7 feet(2134 mm).

100percentliving

Living the House

Architects and designers have, at least in theory, consistently striven to incorporate the occupiers of their buildings into their broader aesthetic and social discourses. However, even the most benign of Modernist visions, whereby inhabitants are offered a functional, blank canvas to "work on" or a "machine to live in" are actually impositions arising from a fraught power relation between the visions of designers and users. With the exception, perhaps, of "signature" buildings commissioned specifically by a patron to express the stylistic intentions of the architect (and of course their own wealth and taste), the majority of people inhabit living spaces in which they have little or no say over the way in which the buildings impose upon them everyday.

The area of architectural design where this "imposition" is most readily acknowledged is that of social housing where the intersection of economics, politics and social reform is at its most transparent. As the historiography of social housing reveals, architects concretise (in many cases quite literally) contemporary socio-political assumptions; from how "working class" people use the bathroom to definitions of "communal" space and beyond.

Of course, there have been extensive critiques of the authoritarian architect imposing their top-down ideologies on the passive inhabitant, one of the recent historical outcomes of which has been the rise in "community" based housing projects where residents' opinions are incorporated into the design process. Such initiatives, while being good intentioned and highly successful, often amount to little more than aesthetic exercises in allowing choice over the colour of window frames or the other such "extras and add-ons" intended to counter the potential alienation of the inhabitants. It is perhaps unsurprising to find then, that one of the most widely publicised and visited social housing projects, which responded to the intentions of community housing initiatives of the 1970s and 80s, is also that most vilified by the architectural profession. The well-known (notorious some might have it), brightly coloured, wobbly-windowed Hundertwasser Haus apartment project in Vienna, Austria, is regarded by many in the profession as a farce, a denial of architectural seriousness, in that its attempts to counter the alienation of social housing are entirely cosmetic. Yet, at least anecdotally, it is one of the most sought after addresses in the city in terms of social housing occupancy, and in keeping with the gentrification of social housing projects in cities across Europe by the cultural elite, it may yet undergo a revisionist interpretation within the architectural/design profession itself! In terms, then, of its consumption by its inhabitants, and the general public as tourists, it seems to have found an entirely different meaning as a consumed and lived building to that espoused within formal canons of architectural taste.

Debates around the disjuncture in intentions between the architect and the user are understandably prominent in the highly politicised arena of social housing. Yet even studies in this well theorised area generally fail to consider how residential buildings are actually "lived" or consumed by the inhabitants and how they generate their own "biographies." How, for example, do the aesthetics and imaginings of the dweller intersect with those of the architecture? The few studies that do exist tend to explore how an architectural masterpiece has "fallen" to its users (Boudin 1985.) Yet it is only in the process of being lived, in an anthropological sense, that a house becomes architecturally realised; and this process rarely has any connection with the intentions of the architects themselves.

The first observation to make is that architecture most frequently inhabits the hiatus between the lived and the imagined. In an ethnographic study of a north London street in England, previous research has shown how significant the imagination of an "ideal," imaginary dwelling has on the lived experience of the "real" dwelling (Clarke 2001.) The resident of a semi-detached 1930s house, for example, had an alternative fisherman's Devonshire cottage in mind when choosing the gingham curtains for the living room. Although she lived on a busy urban road, within the comparably ample proportions of 1930s modern suburban architecture, she lived the sound of the sea and the cosiness of a low ceiling stone walled cottage.

Similarly, Belinda, the owner-occupier of a converted Victorian apartment, with barely enough room to house the furniture of her previous marital relationship, kept an enormous, wrought-iron candelabra (given as a wedding present) as a reminder of the stately baronial home she imagined she might one day have occupied with her husband. Although occasionally filled with church candles for dinner parties, the unwieldy over-ornamented piece dripped wax over the stripped pine floors of Belinda's floors as if, she said, to "mock the humbleness of her real home."

Belinda's neighbours, a couple proud of their unerring Modernist taste, had tried in vain to turn their Edwardian four-bedroom house into a haven of Scandinavian minimalism. After ten years, however, they had finally given up the haunting vision of the Modernist ideal after realising the impracticality of Arne Jacobsen cutlery and being lured into buying floral tablecloths and decorative china to match their Edwardian kitchen; "our taste just fell apart!" they explained.

Further along the street, a mother of three young children, living in a cramped one-bedroom maisonette, talks of "her" cottage in Southern Ireland and its enormous eat-in kitchen and rambling garden; ideal for the country life she imagines for her children. However, "baking home-made cookies," she laughs, is the closest she has come to yet to her "Southern Irish cottage life."

Such imaginings of the ideal home, most frequently expressed in very specific architectural typologies (such as cottage, castle, Modernist house, loft space, etc.) might seem to belie a discontent in keeping with the onset of advanced consumer society. But they are more than empty longings plucked from the pages of lifestyle magazines. They are ideals which embody broader aspirations such as sociality, quality of life or "good" mothering. For architectural forms are lived not just as status symbols, pure space or signifiers, but rather as the melding of human ritual, life cycles and social worlds and trajectories.

The phenomenal growth, over the last decade, in media focused on home-making and gardening has been noted by numerous academics and is most often viewed as symptomatic of the increasingly privatised nature of modern life and the significance of home ownership within capitalism (Birdwall-Pheasant and Lawrence Zúñiga 1999; Gurney 1999; Tomlinson 1990.) While property booms in the western economies have surely fuelled the growth in fantasies and practical projects anchored to the home, the increasing commodification of living space is not the sole explanation for the weight it now carries in everyday culture.

How, for example, do these fantasies around ideal homes equate with the lived experience of inhabitants of state housing whose relation to their architectural living space is bound by non-choice and non-ownership? Is the relevance of such fantasies merely related to those able to enact, even in a limited sense, some choice over their living space and its potential commoditisation as a saleable asset? The following ethnographic example explores how, state housing, as a highly standardised form of architecture, is consumed in the previously described hiatus between the lived and the ideal?

Kelly, a single black British woman with two children, is fully aware of the stigmas, in British society, attached to living in state housing and being a single mother, yet she is possibly as far from being alienated from her living space as is possible. Over the ten years of inhabiting a state housing complex in north London, she has decorated her home to make it an immaculate monochrome interior design worthy of the lifestyle pages of Hello! gossip magazine. As has been shown in other studies of state housing (Miller 1988) it is not unusual for inhabitants to entirely disguise and adapt the original fittings and structures of state housing despite reaping no monetary benefits from this practice and even risking prosecution or eviction from the authorities. But the extent of Kelly's interior design work operates in direct relation to her desire to disassociate herself from state housing, and its social stigmas manifest in the ugly standardisation of its material forms. She uses the unique appropriation of her particular apartment, through the use of unusually glamorous interior design (which notably confines the children's material presence strictly to their bedrooms) to create what she describes as "an oasis" within the housing complex. This interior scheme, however, is also part of a broader aspiration to find a new partner through the creation of a home "fitting enough" to entertain (male) guests. Kelly combines the continual project of home decoration with visits to up-market wine bars where she might find the "man of her dreams" and eventually start a new life outside the social housing estate and its broader strictures; in an ideal private four-bedroom house with a garden for the children.

Aesthetically or otherwise, Kelly's apartment is entirely unrelated to that envisioned or designed by the architect, and no amount of user or focus group research could elicit the immense complexity of any single inhabitant and their relation to the building. However, her strategising to use an ideal, luxurious interior design scheme, in which the adult entertaining space predominates, exists in total opposition to the concrete aesthetic and family home lay-out imposed by the architects. Kelly lives her house as a potential "way out" of social housing. Her habitation of the building consists of a conscious opposition to the State and its architects. This not just as an aesthetic exercise or a means of appropriating the space, but rather a means of developing a trajectory which, from its place in her imagination and everyday practice, might eventually secure a place in a private domestic residence.

The living of houses then is not just an aesthetic or expressive process, but an essentially political practice. The work of archaeologists Buchli and Lucas (2000) reveals how the material culture of a house and its ensuing social relations also become inscribed into the trajectories of the "lived house." Their particular study also considers the home of a single mother living in British state housing. But unlike Kelly and her proactive involvement with her apartment, the individual considered in Buchli

and Lucas' example is entirely absent; her living of the house is evidenced only in the remains material remains of her relations with her two children whom she left behind when vacating the residence in haste. Using an archaeological methodology, they try to piece together the remains of the "lived house." Children's toys and shoes are scattered across the living room floor well as other intimate paraphernalia of child/mother relations. A "baby book" charting the fondest moments of a child's development as well as children's artwork attached to the refrigerator are left behind, so hurried was the departure of the occupants. Remnants of Flintstone wallpaper in child's room and other such details show how carefully the flat was constructed to the taste of the children. Following further research into documentary evidence, it becomes apparent that the mother abandoned her home after the drug addicted, estranged father became threatening towards the family. However, as she has officially "voluntarily" vacated state housing, and left no forwarding address, the anonymous woman will no longer be entitled to state housing. After all, what "good mother," according to general ideology and state legality would give up the bricks and mortar of home so readily, despite the fact that, as the archaeology of the "lived house's" personal effects show the occupant lived up to every definition of being a "good mother." The construction of home and stability is so inextricably tied, in our culture, to definitions of good mothering that, in the face of all evidence to the contrary, this absent mother is condemned and punished by a potential lifetime of homelessness. The architecture of the state, ideologically and materially, enforces such concepts and for those who inhabit it, it has very "real" consequences.

Ideologically loaded notions such as "good mother" may, as the above example reveals, become formalised in external structures such as the state and intimate arenas such as the home and its objects. But how do looser cultural definitions such as "gayness" manifest themselves in the lived house?

In the analysis of previous ethnographic studies, I have shown how consumption practices around provisioning (in the context of fine wines, classic cars and second-hand fashion) are used to "rehearse" certain skills and knowledges in the construction of specific types of masculinity (Clarke 1998). Could the process of living a house be considered in a similar way in terms of a specific rendering of masculinity or sexuality? The following case study considers how a middle class couple live their house vicariously by self-consciously adopting the aesthetic scheme and knowledges of the previous, gay, occupants of their house.

Isolde and Alistair are relatively recent residents on the north London street used as an ethnographic site for the studies previously mentioned in this chapter. Unlike most inhabitants on the street they are unusually well-versed in matters of aesthetics as they are both qualified architects. However, both describe themselves as suffering from an "identity crisis" as they have moved from a loft apartment overlooking a canal, in an up-and-coming working-class area of central London, to an Edwardian semi-detached house in an area they refer to as "utterly non-descript." Forced to vacate their previously rented loft-space, as the owner was selling the property, the couple decided to purchase this house (due to its comparative inexpensiveness) and enjoy its extensive garden. Despite owning the property and enjoying the new-found space of the garden, the informants mock the "twee" architecture of the Edwardian house, even though they recognise that in

general terms it is an extremely desirable property as it has been "lovingly restored" and retains many of its original features.

Putting it simply, Isolde and Alistair are embarrassed by their house. It is fast becoming a social burden. The architectural and design based peer group with whom they socialise mainly live in re-appropriated office or factory spaces in urban areas. Edwardian houses are the antithesis of all they have shared in educational and taste terms.

This couple, then, are having extreme difficulties in "living their house" even after a year of inhabiting it. It seems to be a process of extreme and constant confrontation. Isolde's modern art works do not match the décor. Alistair's Breuer chair and Le Corbusier chaise longue look dreadful in the floral wallpapered lounge. Both seek refuge in a relatively aesthetically safe place, the garden; but even there, the previous occupants have planted some particularly tasteless papyrus grass!

All, however, is not lost as the couple gradually develop a counter aesthetic to incorporate the house into their social worlds. The house's almost oppressive nature, with its dark blue carpets, meticulously applied wall stencilling, and ornate glasswork, is explained away as the previous occupants' taste; and most importantly that it is the work of an extremely successful, wealthy gay couple. Not only have Isolde and Alistair decided to keep the previous occupants' home-improvement schemes (a mosaic walk-in shower room) and decorative features (such as a painted ceiling in one of the bedrooms), ultimately they relish and celebrate them. It is without irony that they also inform friends of their decision to keep the previous couples' gardener and cleaner; though as Isolde points out, the cleaner has far less work to do now with "all of the boys' knick-knacks gone."

The re-invention of this genteel Edwardian semi-detached property as a re-appropriated "gay house" is a precarious means of generating cultural capital. Isolde and Alistair simultaneously draw on some crude stereo-typing of "gay" taste by alluding to some "deeper," "innate" and admirable ability of gay couples to make "a proper home" (whereas they are just tasteful architects.)

These cases show the precarious nature of the house as a lived entity, that whilst the machinations between its four walls might appear to be private it is always part of a broader moral economy; a social object which not only shelters social subjects but is made by them and in turn makes them.

Houses, then, do not just have implications for their users in terms of their aesthetics or symbolic significations. When inhabitants come to occupy architecture they embark on a process in which exchanges between themselves and the preordained nature of their building takes on an agency of its own (Latour 1993.)

The idea that space, material culture and houses are separate entities from their users is a predominantly Western concept, which lends itself to the idea that the task of making a house liveable is purely the domain of the architect. Yet as numerous anthropological studies elucidate (Waterson 1997; Hoskins 1998) the design of a house and its objects is made materially and socially through the melding of social relations, life cycles, traditions of material culture and aesthetics. The formal aesthetics of the branded, signature building tied to a named architect is perhaps then, the least interesting aspect of architectural practice unless it truly considers the anthropology of its inhabitants. For, it is only in the process of "living the house" that the true aesthetic of a building is made; by the occupants themselves.

Alison J. Clarke
London, 2003

Alison J. Clarke is a Professor of Design History and Theory at the University of Applied Arts Vienna. She is also Senior Scholar at the AHRB Centre for the Study of the Domestic Interior at the Royal College of Art, London where she directs a research project titled "Setting Up Home: the Making of the Modern Interior."

References:

Birdwall-Pheasant, D. and D. Lawrence Zúñiga (1999) House Life: Space, Place and Family in Europe, Oxford: Berg.

Boudin, P. (1985) Pessac de Le Corbusier: Etude socio-architecturale, 1929-1985.

Buchli, V. & Lucas, G., (2000) 'Children, gender and the material culture of domestic abandonment in the late twentieth century' in ed. J S. Derevenski, ed. Children and Material Culture, London: Routledge.

Clarke, A. J. (2001) 'The Aesthetics of Social Aspirations' in Home Possessions: Material Culture Behind Closed Doors ed. Daniel Miller, Berg: Oxford.

Clarke, A. J. (1998) 'Window shopping at home: classifieds, catalogues and new consumer skills'. In D. Miller (ed) Material Cultures: Why Some Things Matter. Chicago: University of Chicago Press.

Friedman, A. (1998) Women and The Making of the Modern House: A Social and Architectural History. New York: Harry N. Abrams.

Gurney, C. (1999) 'Lowering the drawbridge: a case study of analogy and metaphor in the social construction of home ownership'. Urban Studies 36/10: 1705-22.

Hoskins, J. (1998) Biographical Objects; How Things Tell the Stories of People's Lives. Routledge

Latour, B. (1993) We Have Never Been Modern. New York: Harvester Wheatsheaf

Miller, D (1987) Mass Consumption and Material Culture. Oxford: Blackwell

Miller, D. (1988) 'Appropriation of the State on the Council Estate'. Man 23: 353-72.

Tomlinson, A. (1990) 'Home fixtures: doing it yourself in a privatised world.' In A. Tomlinson (ed.) Consumption, Identity and Style. London: Comedia.

Van de Hoorn, M. 2003 (in press) 'Consuming the 'Platte' in East Berlin The new popularity of former GDR architecture', Home Cultures. 1/1.

Waterson, R. (1997) The Living House: An Anthropology of Architecture in South East Asia. Thames and Hudson

Wigley, M. (1996) White Walls, Designer Dresses. MIT

when	2002
where	mödling – austria
client	baumgartner
quantity	1
altitude above sea level	246.30 m
coordinates	48° 05' n 16° 16' e
weight	372.70 tons
total payload	61.45 tons
capacity	5 persons
construction time	3405h45min
security options	middle

when	2001
where	gablitz – austria
client	reiger-frischmann
quantity	1
altitude above sea level	284.30 m
coordinates	48° 13' n 16° 09' e
weight	25.30 tons
total payload	4.10 tons
capacity	4 persons
construction time	245h55min
security options	low

bath citronic

when	2000
where	wiener neustadt – austria
client	rewe – bipa parfumerien gesmbh
quantity	3
altitude above sea level	270.20 m
coordinates	47° 48' n 16° 14' e
weight	44.50 tons
total payload	11.20 tons
capacity/flat	2 persons
construction time	342h12min
security options	low

when	1999
where	vienna – austria
client	petrovic
quantity	1
altitude above sea level	161.90 m
coordinates	48° 15' n 16° 25' e
weight	577.30 tons
total payload	65.75 tons
capacity	7 persons
construction time	1441h53min
security options	high

when	2002
where	vienna – austria
client	private
quantity	1
altitude above sea level	172.35 m
coordinates	48° 10' n 16° 20' e
weight	1978.50 tons
total payload	405.20 tons
capacity	8 persons
construction time	4212h30min
security options	high

modification house V

1.1 incidental use areas. spaces which are incidental to the main occupancy shall be separated or protected, or both, in accordance with table 302.

in each story, the building area shall be such that the sum of the ratios of the floor area of each use divided by the allowable area for each use shall exceed one. exception: except for group h and i- 2 areas, where the building is equipped throughout with an automatic sprinkler system, installed in accordance with section 903.3.

306.3 factory industrial- 2 low- hazard occupancy. factory industrial uses that involve the fabrication or manufacturing of noncombustible materials which during finishing, packing or processing do not involve a significant fire hazard

2. liquefied compressed gases are gases that, in a packaging under the charged pressure, are partially liquid at a temperature of 68° f(20° c).

division 1.1. explosives that have a mass explosion hazard. a mass explosion is one which affects almost the entire load instantaneously. division

1. is ignitable at 14.7 psi (101 kpa) when in a mixture of 13 percent or less by volume with air; or 2.

flammable range at 14.7 psi (101 kpa) with air of at least 12 percent, regardless of the lower limit. the limits specified shall be determined at 14.7 ps (101 kpa) of pressure and a temperature of 68° f(20° c) in accordance with astm e 681.

100percentvisions

when	2000
where	norway – competition award
client	city government of oslo
quantity	1
altitude above sea level	4.20 m
coordinates	59° 54' n 10° 43' e
weight	approx. 67.000 tons
total payload	approx. 24500 tons
capacity	approx.1400 persons
security options	high

when	2003
where	graz – austria
client	interio
quantity	1
altitude above sea level	350.30 m
coordinates	47° 04' n 15° 26' e
weight	approx. 9800 tons
total payload	approx. 9000 tons
capacity	1200 persons
construction time	approx. 3000h
security options	high

when	1999 – 2000
where	austria – competition 1. prize
client	government of austria
altitude above sea level	variable
coordinates	47° 20' n 13° 20' e
weight	approx. 750 tons
total payload	approx. 500 tons
capacity	30 persons
security options	high

asfinag (austrian trucking toll authorities)

when	1998
where	linz – austria – competition
client	linz – austria
quantity	1
altitude above sea level	255.30 m
coordinates	48° 18' n 14° 18' e
weight	approx. 16600 tons
total payload	approx. 5500 tons
capacity	1500 persons
construction time	approx. 20800 h
security options	high

lentos museum linz – new gallery

when	1999
where	austria
client	keba linz
altitude above sea level	variable
weight	approx. 0.30 tons
total payload	0.15 tons
capacity	1 person
construction time	2h00min
security options	high

think tank

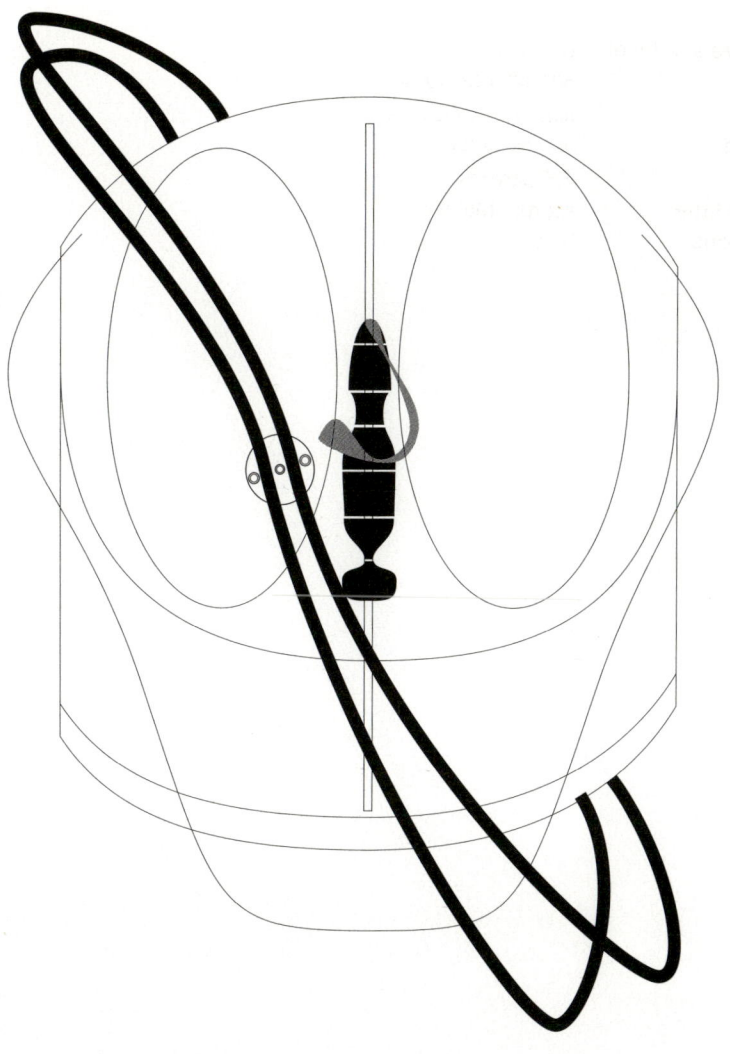

when	1994
where	berlin – germany – competition
client	federal republic of germany
quantity	1
altitude above sea level	68.20 m
coordinates	52° 32' n 13° 22' e
weight	approx. 16.000 tons
total payload	approx. 4000 tons
capacity	400 persons
construction time	approx. 19500h
security options	high

office of the federal president berlin

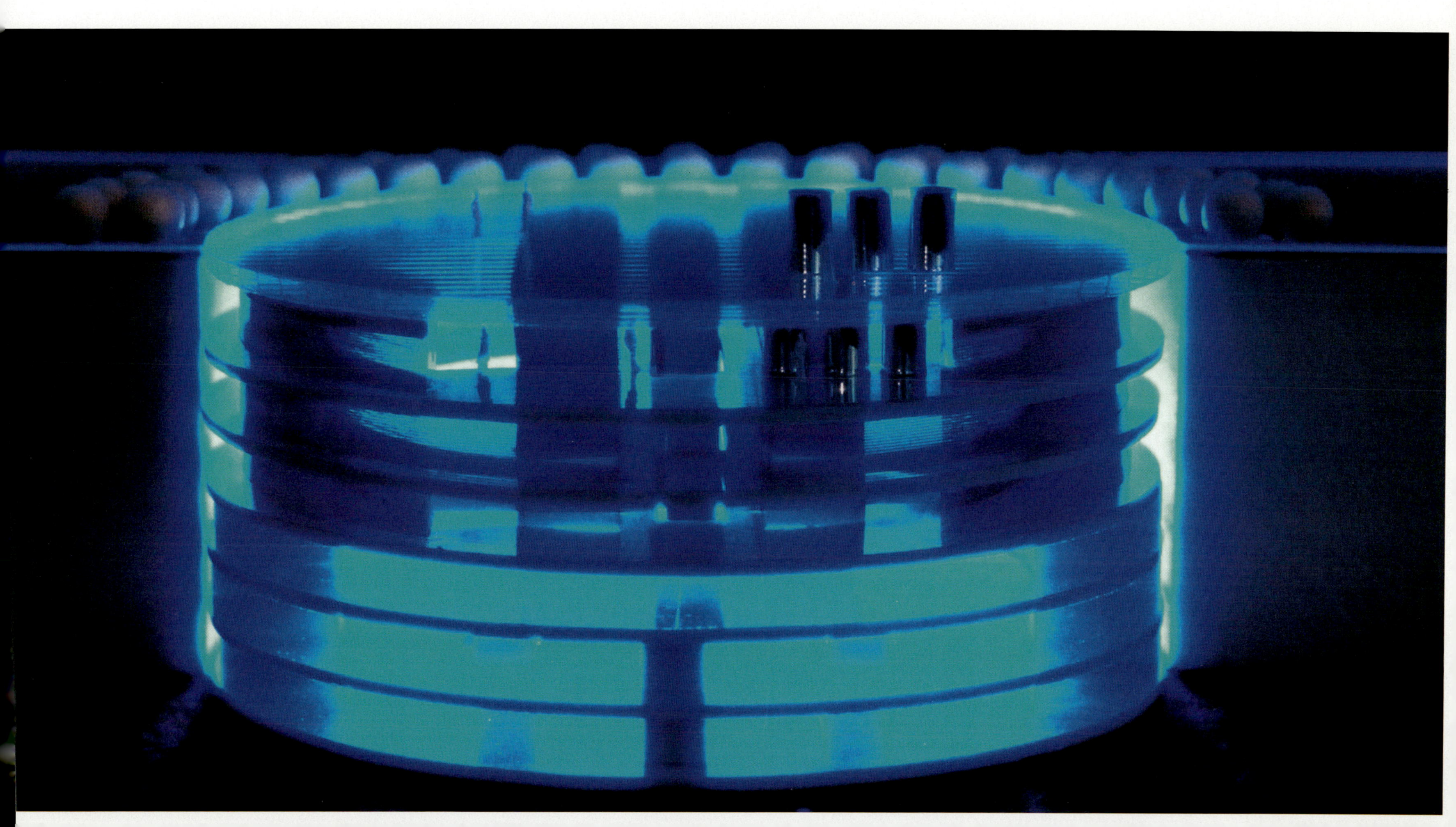

when	2002
where	vienna – austria – competition
client	fair hotel
quantity	1
altitude above sea level	171.20 m
coordinates	48° 15' n 16° 25' e
weight	approx. 12350 tons
total payload	approx. 5700 tons
capacity	approx. 500 persons
security options	high

fair hotel prater

when	1992
where	new york – united states of america – competition 4th prize
client	federal ministry of foreign affairs
quantity	1
altitude above sea level	22.30 m
coordinates	40° 42' n 74° 00' e
weight	approx. 3550 tons
total payload	approx. 1160 tons
capacity	300 persons
construction time	approx. 31200 h
security options	high

austrian cultural forum new york

THE UNIT STAFF 1996 – 2003 and their spontaneous associations with the office

Karoline Aichholzer	since	05/00	"unpretentious"
Wolfgang Bürgler	since	01/96	"unlimited"
Franz Freudenthaler	since	09/96	"professional"
Markus Hasawenth	since	03/03	"casual"
Patrick Hofmann	since	01/96	"unbounded"
Herbert Janker	since	02/99	"chilly"
Christian Jonak	since	06/98	"trendsetting"
Robert Kainzbauer	since	09/99	"photo-technical"
Chira Khanakah	since	01/99	"sovereign"
Johannes Kraut	since	10/98	"stylish"
Clemens Mayer	since	12/01	"straight"
Alexander Nemmert	since	02/02	"crystal clear"
Sascha Niemann	since	01/96	"fast"
Eva Oszter	since	02/03	"dynamic"
Andreas Petrovic	since	01/96	"endless"
Georg Petrovic	since	01/96	"fast"
Christian Pistauer	since	10/01	"straight curve"
Daniela Preißegger	since	10/00	"bright"
Peter Reindl	since	01/96	"unmistakable"
Rainer Repper-Braun	since	11/00	"refreshing"
Ulrike Salchegger	since	02/99	"resolute"
Michael Schmidle	since	09/99	"uni{t}versal"
Romana Schweng	since	07/02	"lucid"
Richard Smertnik	since	05/98	"worldwide"
Wolfgang Weinhäupl	since	05/00	"fun-tastic"
Christian Weinhäupl	since	08/98	"communicative"
Michael Wimberger	since	10/99	"convincing"
Matthias Zawischa	since	07/01	"silky, yet rough"

FORMER STAFFERS

Christopher Aichinger	09/01 – 06/03
Mydia Arif	03/99 – 12/00
Holst Behrens	04/99 – 03/00
Willy Bisschop	12/98 – 12/99
Ingrid Böck	01/97 – 06/99
Thomas Breier	11/00 – 04/03
Hermann Haider	05/99 – 08/02
Andreas Haiderer	01/96 – 04/98
Stefan Hillepold	05/94 – 12/98
Martin Jurycz	09/01 – 10/02
Clemens Kanonier	11/00 – 09/02
Simone Konzett	10/99 – 05/00
Beate Lechner	03/96 – 02/99
Ivana Liovic	07/01 – 09/02
Piet Ploetzer	07/01 – 09/01
Gregor Radinger	11/01 – 06/03
Dieter Schöllnberger	09/01 – 05/02
Alexander Schranz	01/99 – 06/03
Marie-Theres Süssner	06/99 – 02/00

We like to thank our cooperation partners for their work and for supporting

superdiscount

folien wagner, sierndorf
altexa lüftungstechnische anlagen gmbh, wien
alu könig stahl gmbh, wien
alu suisse austria gmbh wien
arneg kühlmöbel und ladeneinrichtungen gmbh, leonding
bene büromöbel kg, wien
besam maschinenhandels gmbh, wien
brucha gmbh, wien
brüder assmann gmbh, wien
brüder eckelt + co. glastechnik gmbh, steyr
c. peters baugmbh, linz
construction support baugmbh, wien
dorma aks automatic gmbh, biedermannsdorf
eder reinhard blechbau gmbh, völkermarkt
erhartmaier innenausbau und sanierungs gmbh, gratkorn
ernst seidl segelmacherei, salzburg
et lettera werbegestaltungs gmbh, wien
franye gmbh, bad sauerbrunn
gerflor gmbh, hörsching
gradwohl gmbh, melk
haironville austria gmbh, leobersdorf
hali büromöbel gmbh, wien
hauser kühlanlagen gmbh&co kg, linz
inform tischlerei gmbh, feldkirchen
klotzner sonnenschutztechnik gmbh, linz
licht loidl gmbh, lafnitz
lichthaus haid gmbh, innsbruck
malerei kara gmbh, bad vöslau
malex gmbh, bad st. leonhard
menerga energie-systeme gmbh, wien
nessl fliesen gmbh, spittal/drau
plakativ x-large printing, wien
pyromax, manus p.m.t. feuerlöschgeräte gmbh, wien
reifetshammer bedachungen gmbh, wels
reisenhofer haustechnik kg, gleisdorf
riegler metallbau gmbh, steyr
scheybal matten gmbh, wien
sensormatic sicherheitstechnik gmbh, bergheim
siteco beleuchtungstechnik gmbh, wien
stagro schumi straßenmarkierungen gmbh, salzburg
steco baugmbh, oberwart
steiner mediensysteme gmbh, leobersdorf
technoholz gmbh, villach
glaserei thinius gmbh, wien
tischlerei wegerer gmbh, rettenegg
toro bausanierungs- u. handelsgmbh, wien
trevision großbildtechnik gmbh, pottendorf
typico megaprints gmbh, lochau
umdasch shop concept gmbh, wien
unger stahlbau gmbh, oberwart
villeroy & boch austria handelsgmbh, linz
vitra büromöbel gmbh, wien
vola armaturen vertriebs gmbh, leibnitz
vorwerk teppiche austria gmbh, hard
xs42 ltd graphik, wien
xsigns design, wien
zumtobel licht gmbh, wien

bibliography

Awards and Prizes
2001 2nd prize Städtebauliche Entwicklung Aspern
2000 Award: Oslo Opera House – International Competition
2000 4th prize Betriebsstätten Klagenfurt (ASFINAG)
1998 1st Prize: 200 ASFINAG toll booths across Austria
1995 Honorary Mention: Deutscher Architekturpreis
1995 Nomination: Staatspreis für Wirtschafts-, Gewerbe- und Industriebauten
1994 Client's Award: Preis der Zentralvereinigung österreichischer Architekten
1994 1st prize Rathaus Rainbach, Oberösterreich
1993 Honorary Mention: Kärntner Landesbaupreis
1993 4th prize Montanuniversität Leoben
1993 2nd prize Elektrotechnisches Institut Graz
1992 4th Prize: Austrian Cultural Institute in New York –
     international competition in cooperation with Fritz Weber

Exhibitions
2001 "Metamorphosen des Raumes im 20. Jahrhundert" in Weimar, Berlin, Stuttgart und Aachen (D) -
     Wanderausstellung mit Symposium
2000 "Den Norske Opera" in der Gallerie Antonella Nicola Turin (I) – Wettbewerb Opernhaus Oslo
2000 "Den Fuß in der Tür" - Manifeste junger österr. Architekten, Künstler u. Literaten zum Thema "Das
     ideale Wohnen in der Stadt" im Künstlerhaus Wien (A)
1999 "New Austrian Architecture" im Ringturm Wien (A)
1999 Architektur Zentrum Wien – Architektur Archiv Austria (Internet) www.azw.at/D
     Raum aktueller Kunst – "Emotion – Klang" Wien

Books and Catalogs
Österreichische Architektur in New York, Hrsg. Ernst Bliem (Verlag Haymon) 1993

Internationales Jahrbuch f. Licht und Architektur, Hrsg. Ingeborg Flagge
(Verlag Ernst & Sohn) 1994

Internationales Jahrbuch f. Licht und Architektur, Hrsg. Ingeborg Flagge
(Verlag Rudolf Müller) 2000

Architecture for the Work Environment – Neue Bauten für Industrie und Gewerbe
in Österreich, Hrsg. Degenhard Sommer, Bernhard Holletschek, Lutz Weißer
(Verlag Birkhäuser) 1995

Innovative Austrian Architecture, Hrsg. Biswas (Springer Verlag) 1996

Architektur in Deutschland, (Karl Krämer Verlag) 1995

la ville sur la ville - die Stadt über der Stadt/Europan 4, Hrsg. Joh. Fiedler, Elke Platzer (Steiermärk.
Landesdruckerei Graz) 1997

Architekturpreis Berlin, Hrsg. Bund Deutscher Architekten Berlin
(Gebr. Mann Verlag Berlin) 1994

AWA 96 Int. Yearbook Award Winning Architecture, (Verlag Prestel) 1996

ORTE – Architektur in Niederösterreich 1986-1997, (Verlag Birkhäuser) 1997
KREMS – Stadt im Aufbruch 99, Architektur und Städtebau eine Bilanz, (Magistrat d. Stadt Krems
Stadtbaudirektion) 1999

Den Fuß in der Tür: Manifeste des Wohnens, Hrsg. Jan Tabor, Künstlerhaus Wien, Kammern der
Architekten und Ingenieurkonsulenten (Verlag Arch+Ing) 2000

DESIGN SECRETS: Office Spaces – 50 real-life projects uncovered, Elana Frankel (Verlag Rockport)
2001

ARCHITEKTUR für Sport, Peter Stürzebecher/Sigrid Ulrich, (Verlag Bauwesen) 2001

Periodicals
Wallpaper (GB/US), Nov. Dez 1998 (64)

Frame (N), 13 März/April 2000 (22)

Le Moniteur Architecture (F), Dec./2000 (62 – 63); Nov. 2001/ (139 – 141);
Dec./2001 (94 – 95)

Interior Design Magazine (USA), Okt. 2001 (142 – 143)

Dwell magazine (USA), Feb. 2002 (43)

Abitare (I), Nr. 399 Okt./00 (217 – 221)

AIT (D), 7-8/95 (58 - 61); 10/98 (120-123); 12/98 (70-75, 124-125); 3/99 (78-81); 12/99 (72-77); 12/00
(158 – 163); 3/02 (136– 137)

Architektura & Biznes (Polen), 9/2001 (50 – 53)

Parnass (Kunst, Architektur, Design) (A), 3/4 – 1999 (50)

Archithese (D), Juni/99 (23)

Stern (D), Nr. 17, 19.04.2000 (152)

Bauwelt (D), 22/95 (1236-1237) ; 34/98 (1875-1877)

Deutsche Bauzeitschrift (D), 5/94 (47 - 54); 5/95 (32-33); "Büro '98" (83-89); 10/99 (55 – 58);
Sonderheft Büro & Architektur 2001

Licht & Architektur (D), 5/1994 (12,13)

Baumeister (D), 4/95 (6); 10/95 (11)

Architektur & Wettbewerbe (D), 180/99 (32-33)

Architektur und Bauforum 2/96; 4/98; 2/00 (26 – 34); 4/00 (72 – 73); 1/2002 (39)

Architektur Aktuell (A), 3/95 (8); 6/98 (110-115); 7-8/99 (158-165);
9/00 (10); 5/01 (102 – 105)

Architekturjournal Wettbewerbe (A), 119 1993, (45); 125 1993, (142); 127 1994 (143); 131 1994 (166);
135-136 1994 (122)

Architektur (A), 12/1994 (52 - 55); 12/98 (46-50); 4/99 (44-48); 8/99 (24-25);
6/00 (6 – 7); 09/00 (51 – 54); 3/01 (58 – 61)

Möbel, Raum, Design (A), 2/1994

B.Ü.R.O. (A), 1/99 (82-84); 1/00 (63); 02/00 (92 – 93)

imprint

the unit
Wolfgang Bürgler and Georg Petrovic, Architects Vienna
www.theunit.at

© 2003 Springer-Verlag/Wien
Printed in Austria

Conception, editorial work
section.a
art.design.consulting GmbH
www.sectiona.at

Graphic Design
section.d
design.communication GmbH
www.sectiond.at

Photographic work
Pascal Petignat
(petignat@re-p.at)

Translation and copy editing
Pedro M. López

Following projects have been realised by "the office"
Merkur D p. 52, Wolford p. 64, Ilbau Headquarter p. 148, Rainbow Collection p. 202,
Billa 2000 p. 68, Central Billa Fresh Specialities Warehouse p. 164,
Bipa (Mariahilferstraße) page 76, Ilbau Technology Park Berlin p. 160,
Competition Cultural Forum New York p. 250

The editor would like to thank the architecture office, the photographers, the graphic designer, the translator and the publishing house for their productive cooperation.

Illustration Credits

Pascal Petignat
Pages: 6, 7, 22, 25, 26, 90, 93, 94, 114, 117, 118, 154, 157, 158, 178, 181, 182, 210, 213, 214

Claudia Bokmeier
Pages: 50, 133, 134, 135

Mischa Erben
Pages: 49, 51

Nikolaus Korab
Pages: 37, 38, 39, 41, 42, 43, 45, 46, 47, 61, 62, 63, 77, 79 (right), 81, 82, 83, 85, 86, 87, 97, 98, 99, 101, 102, 103, 109, 110, 111, 121, 122, 123, 129, 130, 131, 137, 138, 139, 185, 186, 187, 191, 192, 193, 195, 196, 197, 199, 200, 201, 217, 218, 219, 223, 224, 225, 231, 232, 233

Rupert Steiner
Pages: 33, 34, 35, 53, 54, 55, 57, 58, 59, 65, 66, 67, 69, 70, 71, 105, 106, 107, 125, 126, 127, 141, 142, 143, 145, 146, 147, 149, 150, 151, 161 ,162, 163, 165, 166, 167, 169, 170, 171, 173, 174, 175, 189, 203, 204, 205, 221, 227, 228, 229

the unit
Pages: 29, 30, 31, 73, 74, 75, 79 (left), 207, 237, 239, 241, 242, 243, 245, 247, 249, 251

Pyramids © Jonathan Blair/CORBIS page 14
Harrods © Pawel Libera/CORBIS page 15
Skyskrapers Hong Kong © So Hing-Keung/CORBIS page 16
Bank of Amerika © Morton Beebe, S.F./CORBIS page 17
Big Ben / London © Jose Fuste Raga/CORBIS page 18
Winnie the Pooh © John & Dallas Heaton/CORBIS page 19

Printing
Holzhausen Druck & Medien GmbH, A-1140 Wien

Printed on acid-free and chlorine-free bleached paper

SPIN: 10926239

CIP data applied for

With 191 coloured figures

ISBN 3-211-02239-2 Springer-Verlag Wien New York